This Prison Where I Live

The PEN Anthology of Imprisoned Writers

Edited by Siobhan Dowd
Foreword by Joseph Brodsky

CASSELL

Cassell
Wellington House, 125 Strand, London WC2R 0BB
127 West 24th Street, New York, NY 10011

© International PEN 1996

First published 1996

British Library Cataloguing-in-Publication Data
A catalogue record for this book is available from the British Library.

ISBN 0-304-33304-2 (hardback)
      0-304-33306-9 (paperback)

Cover photograph by Leo Divendal

Designed and typeset by Kenneth Burnley at Irby, Wirral, Cheshire.
Printed and bound in Great Britain by Biddles Ltd, Guildford and King's Lynn

Contents

Acknowledgements

I would like to express warmest thanks to the following friends and colleagues whose advice and help during the preparation of this book proved invaluable: Michaela Becker, Alexandre Blokh, Peter Day, Mandy Garner, Jane Greenwood, Ronald Harwood, Marjorie Heins, Robin Jones, Laurie Jonietz, Karen Kennerly, Rose Kernochan, Ann Kjellberg, Jake Kreilkamp, Joanne Leedom-Ackerman, Sandra Margolies, Lamia Matta, Elizabeth Paterson, Michael Scammell, William Schwalbe, Thomas von Vegesack, Sara Whyatt, and Karina Zabihi.

Foreword

Prison is essentially a shortage of space made up for by the surplus of time; to an inmate, both are palpable. Naturally enough, this ratio – echoing man's situation in the universe – is what has made incarceration an integral metaphor of Christian metaphysics as well as practically the midwife of literature. As regards literature, this stands to reason, in a certain sense, since literature is in the first place a translation of metaphysical truths into any given vernacular.

Such translation can be attained of course even without incarceration, and perhaps with greater accuracy. From Paul onward, however, the Christian tradition has been relying on incarceration as a means of revelatory transportation with remarkable consistency. Now, as this book is about to demonstrate, the cultures and literatures based on other creeds and principles (if that is the word) than Christianity are doing their utmost to catch up with their great senior – or, as the case may be *vis-à-vis* the Chinese, junior – hoping no doubt to generate in the process their own Villons and Dostoevskys.

In the twentieth century, imprisonment of writers comes practically with the territory. You can hardly name a language, not to mention a country (Norway, perhaps?), whose writers were fully exempted from the trend. Some languages and countries fared better, of course; others worse. Russia seems to have bested them all; but then, as the USSR, it was a very populous empire. With its demise, the center of this problem's gravity has shifted out of Europe to the far eastern and southern reaches of Asia, to Africa, to the archipelagos of the South Pacific. This is not such good news either since those, too, are extremely populous regions. In its refusal to discriminate, geography seems eager to catch up with history.

Or perhaps it's history catching up with geography. By and large a writer finds himself behind bars for taking sides in the political argument that is a sure sign of history. (The absence of such argument is of course the chief characteristic of geography.) He may even try to comfort himself with this interpretation of his predicament, which by now has acquired the aspect of a noble tradition. However, this interpretation won't last him long in the cell, being too broad for his comfort, or, more accurately, for his discomfort. No matter what historical bell a prison may ring, it always wakes you up – usually at 6 a.m. – to the unpalatable reality of your own term.

It's not that prison makes you shed your abstract notions. On the contrary, it pares them down to their most succinct articulations. Prison is indeed a translation of your metaphysics, ethics, sense of history, etc. into the compact terms of your daily deportment. The most effective place for that is of course solitary, with its reduction of the entire human universe to a concrete rectangle permanently lit by the sixty-watt luminary of its bulb under which you revolve in pursuit of your sanity. After a couple of months of that, the solar system is thoroughly compromised – unlike, hopefully, your friends and close associates – and if you are a poet, you may end up with a few decent lyrics under your belt. Pen and paper are seldom available to a prisoner.

So you are best off with rhyme and meter to make the stuff memorable, especially in view of some interrogation methods that render your output frequently unreliable. On the whole, poets fare better in solitary confinement than do fiction writers, because their dependence on professional tools is marginal: one's recurrent back-and-forth movements under that electric luminary by themselves force the lyric's eventual comeback no matter what. Furthermore, a lyric is essentially plotless and, unlike the case against you, evolves according to the immanent logic of linguistic harmony.

In fact, writing – more exactly, composing in your head – formal poetry may be recommended in solitary confinement as a kind of self-therapy, alongside push-ups and cold ablutions. In a shared cell matters are somewhat different, and by and large a fiction writer fares better than a poet. Prose is admittedly an art rooted in social inter-course, and a fiction writer is quicker to find a common denominator with his cellmates than a poet. Being a story-teller he is curious almost by definition, and this helps him to establish rapport with his fellow prisoners by inquiring about their cases and circumstances as well as treating them to his own or other authors' plots. All along he may be fancying himself gathering material for his future work, or perceived as such by his cellmates, who are only too glad to bestow upon him their own, very often deliberately ornate, accounts of their lives.

As this book shows, he gathers it indeed. The bulk of these pages clearly favors prose. This is not because fiction writers are incarcerated more often than poets (in fact, the reverse seems to be the case). This is above all because poetry finds the monotonous idiom of penal certitude plainly hostile to the abrupt nature of verse. It's not that the art of poetry refuses to honor the base reality of oppression with the flowers of eloquence, although one could put it this way. It's just that the essence of any good lyric is compression and velocity. This is so much so that even when a poet resolves to record his penal experience he as a rule resorts to prose. Be that as it may, a poem about prison is harder to come by – even in modern Russian literature – than a novel, let alone memoirs. Perhaps poetry is the least mimetic of all arts.

If it isn't, then the subject of its mimesis is clearly beyond and above prison walls bristling with barbed wire, guards, machine guns, etc. All art aspires to the condition of music, said Walter Pater, and poetry, for one, apparently refuses to become mesmerized by human suffering, including that of its very practitioners. The natural inference is that there are matters more absorbing than the frailty of one's body or agony of one's soul. This inference made by both the public and its watchdogs makes poetry and all arts dangerous. To put it differently, art's unwitting by-product is the notion that the overall human potential is far greater than can be exercised, not to mention catered to, by any given social context. In certain circles this news is unwelcome, and the wider these circles are the more willingly they tend to square a writer.

Now, a writer is certainly not a sacred cow: he can't be above the law or, for that matter, the lawlessness of his society. A prison or a concentration camp is that society's extension, not foreign territory, although your diet there may suggest that much alone. By finding himself behind bars he just continues to share in his people's predicament. Neither in their eyes – nor, one should hope, in his own – is he any different from them. There is in fact a certain element of dishonesty in trying to spring a writer from a prison filled with his compatriots – as it were, with his readers and subjects. It's like throwing a single life-belt into an overcrowded boat sinking in the sea of injustice. Yet thrown this life-belt must be, because it's better to save one than nobody, and also because, once saved, this one can send a more powerful SOS signal than anyone else in that sinking boat.

That is what this book represents. It is an anthology of SOS transmissions, received or ignored for the better part of this century by the luxury liners which happened to pass through the disaster area.

Although there are plenty of books on our shelves that we will never touch, a life-belt should be thrown to a writer, for the simple reason that he might produce yet another book. For it is to the books on our shelves that we owe the existence of the so-called luxury liners in the first place. The more books sitting on our shelves, the fewer men we put in prisons. Of course, by getting a writer – especially a poet – out of jail, society perhaps deprives itself of some metaphysical breakthrough, but the bulk of its members would readily trade that for the banality of their relative security, no matter in what way the metaphysical truths are obtained. In short, the time spent reading a book is time stolen from acting; and in a world settled as thickly as ours the less we act the better.

As for this book, it is about suffering and endurance. As such, it is of great prurient interest to the general public, which is still bliss-fully in the position of perceiving incarceration as an anomaly. It is in order to make this perception survive in the world to come that this book should be read. For there is nothing more tempting than to suc-cumb to viewing the incarceration of people as the norm, as there is nothing easier than perceiving – and indeed obtaining – spiritual benefits from the experience of incarceration itself.

Man is in the habit of detecting a higher purpose and meaning in manifestly meaningless reality. He has a tendency to treat the hand of authority as an albeit blunt instrument of providence. An overall sense of guilt and delayed come-uppance conspire in this attitude to make him easy prey, all along priding itself on attaining new depths of humility. This is an old story, as old as the history of oppression itself, which is to say as old as the history of submission.

But what may be an ascent for a pilgrim is a slippery slope for soci-ety. The world to come is bound to be settled more thickly than this one, and even an anomaly will take on epidemic proportions. There are no penicillins here; the only possible remedy is the home-made, totally individualistic, idiosyncratic deportment of the potential vic-tim. So read this book now as a manual for asserting individualism under overwhelming odds, under extraordinary duress, for writers are, above all and in spite of their convictions or physical frames, individualists. They don't get along with one another, their gifts and stylistic devices differ greatly; they are also guiltier than most people because they are the first for whom repetition compromises words. In other words, a writer is himself a superb metaphor of the human condition. Therefore what he's got to say about imprisonment should be of great interest to those who fancy themselves free.

Ultimately this book may help to dispel some of the prison mystique. In the popular mind prison is the unknown and thus enjoys a close proximity to death, which is the ultimate in the unknown and in the deprivation of freedom. Initially at least, solitary confinement can be compared to a coffin without much hesitation. Allusions to the netherworld in a discourse on prisons are commonplace in any vernacular – unless such discourse is simply taboo. For as regards a standard human reality, prison is indeed an afterlife, structured as intricately and implacably as any ecclesiastical version of the kingdom of death, and by and large rich in grey hues.

However, a partial deprivation of freedom – which is what a prison is – is worse than the absolute one, since the latter cancels your ability to register this deprivation. Further, in prison you are not at the mercy of some unpalpable demons, but in the hands of your own kind, whose tactility is excessive. It's quite possible that the bulk of netherworld imagery in our culture derives precisely from the penal experience.

In any case, this book shows you that hell is both man-made and manned by man. Herein lies your prospect for enduring it, since men, cruel as they are paid to be, are negligent, corruptible, lazy, and so on. No man-made system is perfect, and the system of oppression is no exception. It is subject to fatigue, to cracks, which you are more likely to discover the longer your term. In other words, there is no point in tempering your convictions this side of the prison wall because you might find yourself behind it. By and large, prisons are survivable. Though hope is indeed what you need least upon entering here: a lump of sugar would be more useful.

JOSEPH BRODSKY
New York, December 1995

Introduction

Having come out of that hell, I know that there is nothing supernatural about it. It is a hell made by one man for another man, and it should be destroyed by man.

(Reza Baraheni, Iranian poet)

Prison and PEN

Prison has come to have many connotations in various societies: punishment by confinement; a place of atonement, discipline or re-education; a sequestered building in which society's dregs can fester, forgotten, behind high walls. Some of prison's advocates may have laudable intentions. Perhaps they believe there is no other way to protect society from its worst elements. Perhaps, despite statistics on recidivism, they retain hopes that the rigours of prison routine might have a corrective effect on the inmates' bad morals.

This anthology, however, is not about the locking up of criminals, whatever one thinks of this practice. Instead it examines the misuse of prison, which in this century has been commonplace. In the hands of despots of all political stamps, prison has been the favoured method of silencing dissent. It has been a place where the outspoken critics of repression (often writers) have been locked away and where some of the most barbaric and sadistic of human impulses have had full rein. Small wonder, then, that prison has taken on a terrifying mystique: it is seen as hell on earth. Whole populations will comply with oppressive directives without complaint rather than risk being sent there.

Surviving prison when it is put to this misuse requires integrity and, perhaps more importantly, dogged determination. This anthology is a testament to that doggedness. In these pages the reader will find men and women of great resourcefulness, stretched to the limits of their endurance, but still able to display virtues such as good humour, dignity and philosophical detachment. Many write about the prison world in a way which explodes the clichés. There is more written about boredom, for instance, than torture. Many prefer to meditate on happiness rather than depression. Many, far from being heroes, admit instead to impatience, petty obsessions and greedy self-interest. Yet for all the faults the characters in this book display, one fault is nowhere in evidence: dishonesty. These extracts display candour and a ruthless honesty throughout. Some imprisoned writers have perhaps tended to exaggerate or distort their experiences behind bars. Not the writers in this book. Here the reader will find quiet, collected accounts, chosen specifically for their truthfulness. The last thing the prison mystique needs is perpetuation, and only utter veracity, not hyperbole, can destroy mystiques. These writers are holding up the inequities of the prison world for our clear viewing: only by presenting a scrupulously faithful image, they believe, can the practice of imprisonment for dissent be stamped out.

PEN, the international writers' association, has been working towards the same end since 1921. Now seventy-five years old, the organization has come of age in a time of convulsive global change, yet has survived the Second World War and the Cold War and, so far, the mushrooming of ethnic conflicts in the post-Cold War period. Throughout, PEN has retained its politically neutral identity despite the rise and fall of many left- and right-wing movements. Like any organization, it has had its defining moments, some involving internal struggles. These, however, were its rites of passage, and without them PEN would not have become what it is today: a worldwide association with tens of thousands of writer-members on five continents in over ninety countries, all devoted to defending the freedom of the written word in general and imprisoned writers in particular.

This anthology, then, for all the grimness of its subject matter, is a celebration: it celebrates PEN at seventy-five and the survival of those many writers who have been unjustly imprisoned during these last seventy-five years. There is a third reason for celebration: the efforts of PEN, other human rights groups, and most especially the dissidents themselves, have wrought some progress. Today, there are fewer long-term cases of imprisoned writers than there were even ten years ago. Since the collapse of communism in Europe, there has been a visible decline in the practice of imprisoning dissidents in many countries, although not all. The trend has not gone beyond the point of no return and heightened efforts will be required to ensure its continuance. But a cautious celebration is justified and hence this book.

PEN's work on behalf of imprisoned writers

Throughout the turmoil of the twentieth century, writers have often been among the first to speak out against intolerance and injustice; in many cases they have been in the vanguard of those advocating societal change. Not surprisingly, many have wound up in prison as a result. PEN's unifying mission is their relief. While PEN was not founded with this precise task in mind, it quickly embraced it and indeed became one the world's first human rights organizations. No other organization of writers with PEN's international reach exists; nor can any other human rights group boast PEN's uniquely effective constituency. When freedom of expression comes under attack even in a little-publicized, often-overlooked country, the voices of internationally celebrated writers raised in protest around the globe make no small sound.

PEN's defence of its professional colleagues may seem like self-interest. To some extent it is. However, PEN has always held that preserving the space which writers need to think and create has wider benefits than the welfare of the writers themselves. By defending them, we are also putting a spotlight on the censors and undermining their effectiveness. The censors wish to create silence: PEN wishes to break it.

In short, PEN aims to make imprisonment counter-productive. Nothing captures the international imagination as readily as a writer behind bars. Using this fact, PEN has demonstrated time and again to the world's despots that their action in imprisoning a writer, far from brushing the awkward ideas of that writer under the table, will cause them to be spread across the major newspapers of the world. With the attention for an individual case of a writer in prison comes discussion and understanding of the importance of upholding freedom of expression in general.

Indeed, one might even argue that PEN's work and advocacy helped *define* freedom of expression within the context of the growing acceptance of universally applicable human rights standards that resulted, in mid-century, in the United Nations' Universal Declaration of Human Rights. This declaration states:

Everybody shall have the right to freedom of opinion and expression; this right includes freedom to hold opinions without interference and to seek, receive, and impart information and ideas through any media and regardless of frontiers.

3

Those who wrote these words understood, as PEN members such as H. G. Wells (who incidentally helped to draft the language of these new international covenants) had already, that freedom of expression is not a luxury: it is rather a right on which other rights depend. It is the oxygen without which a healthy, free society cannot flourish. In its absence, other rights, even the right to life, can go by the wayside. Tyrants use censorship to create the silence with which they screen their worst atrocities – even genocide. The silence protects them from accountability.

So, if we are to avoid the horrors of the twentieth century in the twenty-first century, we must protect freedom of expression, a fundamental human right, more avidly than ever before.

PEN's history

Amy Dawson Scott, known universally as 'Sappho', was an idealistic and irrepressible woman, a vibrant and beloved figure of literary London in the 1920s. Although not herself a writer of the first rank, she founded PEN (*P*oets, *E*ssayists, *N*ovelists, later to be expanded to Poets, Playwrights, Essayists, Editors, Novelists) in 1921. This was not the only club she had experimented with: she joked in one letter to her daughter that a Tarot card reader had dubbed her the 'queen of clubs'. But it was the one that took off because its central tenet – the notion of internationalism – truly hit a chord with the prominent writers of the day.

Internationalism was the driving force of her concept. Even after the appalling blood-letting and pointlessness of the First World War, national hatreds were still rife, and fears of renewed war led to the founding of many institutions dedicated to promoting mutual understanding between nations. Foremost of these was the League of Nations. Sappho's original thought appears to have been less grandiose. Her aim was simply to provide foreign writers with a warm reception when they visited London. A recent trip by the American novelist Edith Wharton to London had occurred, she felt, in something of a vacuum. She told her daughter that her aim in founding PEN was to avoid such a lack of response in the future, and to build an international club whose writer-members would be sure of a welcome wherever they went.

Early members included John Galsworthy, the first president, Joseph Conrad, G. K. Chesterton, John Masefield, Arnold Bennett,

E. M. Forster, and H. G. Wells, the second president. Virginia Woolf turned down an invitation to join, apparently seeing the group as yet another dining club. George Bernard Shaw, however, who hesitated for three years before joining, was eventually won over by the emergence of PEN's identity as an international organization with high ideals.

PEN's swift growth was what preoccupied the executive committee members in early days. Centres were quick to spring up in Europe and America. In 1923, the minutes of PEN's executive committee reveal that there was even an idea of starting up a Russian PEN which would contain both *emigré* and resident writers; however, an enquiry to Gorky, among others, revealed that this was not possible at the time (a Russian PEN was not to be founded, in the event, until 1988).

The first glimmer of PEN's human rights mission came in 1932 at the Hungarian Congress, where a resolution was unanimously passed opposing the suppression of literature. 'The protest is made by the PEN,' the resolution declared, 'without regard to political considerations, but entirely in the interests of literature and in loyalty to the principle that the thoughts of authors worthy of the name should be given complete freedom of expression.'

The following year saw a dramatic upheaval within the organization. At the Congress in Dubrovnik, tempers became frayed when there was an attempt by the German PEN to prevent Ernst Toller, a German Jew who had been forced to leave Germany with the rise of Nazism, from speaking. A bitter argument followed during which PEN had an identity crisis: was the organization first and foremost a club, faithful to its members, or a movement, faithful to principles, still themselves waiting to be defined? A resolution obliquely condemning the burning of books in Nazi Germany had been passed at the Congress the day before; the overwhelming mood was to stay true to principle. The vote was passed to let Toller speak. The German PEN walked out in disgust.

The first resolutions for imprisoned writers were passed at the Catalan Congress of May 1935; one, presented by the PEN American Center and seconded by the English centre, concerned a jailed Haitian author, Jacques Roumain. 'From the information received,' the resolution stated, 'it would appear that an error of justice has been made.' The government of Haiti was asked to reconsider the case. The other resolution called for the release of Ludwig Ronn and Carl Ossietzky in Germany.

From then on, discussion of cases in such countries as Argentina, Spain, and Germany became a frequent hallmark of the executive committee meetings. In 1937, a telegram on behalf of Frederico Garcia Lorca was dispatched. Unhappily it arrived too late; he was executed soon after his arrest. At the next PEN Congress, held in Paris in June of that year, a French-sponsored resolution was passed rendering homage to his memory and informing the Spanish people of the shock felt by so terrible an assault on the world of letters. A happier result came from PEN's advocacy on behalf of Arthur Koestler, a Hungarian-born journalist and novelist who was arrested in Spain soon after Lorca and condemned to death. PEN's international appeal on his behalf was apparently noted by his captors: his death sentence was quashed and he was released.

During the Second World War, PEN's international meetings were put on hold, but the organization mounted large-scale relief operations to assist the many writers who found themselves in penurious exile. In 1949, a resolution submitted by the PEN American Center was passed which expressed PEN's wish to be 'representative of the writers of the world' before the newly created United Nations. A representative was designated to attend the meeting of the United Nations Organization in Geneva that July and establish a formal link. PEN did indeed acquire formal consultative status as a result.

Throughout the 1950s, the *ad hoc* efforts on behalf of imprisoned writers continued. These initiatives consisted more often of quiet dialogue than public campaigns. In 1959, a telegram was sent to the Soviet Writers' Union expressing distress at the 'rumors concerning Pasternak' and asking the union to 'protect the poet, and maintain the right of creative freedom. Writers throughout the world are thinking of him fraternally.' Pasternak's ostracism provoked telegrams from PEN centres as remote as Japan and perhaps provided fuel for the 1960 founding of a new standing committee within PEN to focus exclusively on the fate of writers in prison.

The new Writers in Prison Committee consisted in the early days of a few individual members: Rosamond Lehmann, Storm Jameson, Arthur Miller, Paul Tabori, Victor van Vriesland and Peter Elstob were the most prominent activists in the first ten years. The formation of the committee quickly boosted PEN's efforts on behalf of imprisoned writers. The work was more comprehensive and the protests took on a stronger tone. Peter Elstob undertook a special trip to Nigeria on behalf of Wole Soyinka in 1969, where he met quietly with diplomats and government officials. After his trip and a flurry of telegrams from many PEN centres, the minutes of the organization note that 'a report appeared in *The Times* (18 August) that Soyinka was now receiving medical treatment'. The same period saw protests for other luminaries: Vaclav Havel was first defended by PEN in 1970; the resolution on his behalf notes that he was the 'author of the famous Manifesto of 2000 words'. Solzhenitsyn occupied much attention up until the time of his leaving the Soviet Union. And in Greece, many intellectuals, not least the famous poet Yannis Ritsos, were defended.

While the abysmal conditions of writers in communist Eastern Europe occupied much of the Committee's attention from this period until the time of *glasnost*, writers suffering violence and intimidation in Latin America were also causing deep concern. In the 1970s and 1980s, the chair of the Writers in Prison Committee, Michael Scammell, wrote regular reports for PEN's twice-yearly international meetings which summarized the dire state of freedom of expression in most parts of the world. The concentration camps of the period were branded by him as 'welters of human cruelty'.

Scammell's work was taken over in 1987 by the Swedish writer and publisher Thomas von Vegesack. The transition occurred at a turning-point in history: Gorbachev was to meet President Reagan in Reykjavik. As a goodwill gesture, the Russian poet, Irina Ratushinskaya, on whose behalf many PEN centres had worked energetically, was released. After many years of campaigning for Soviet writers to seemingly little effect, her release seemed like the first flicker of hope. *Glasnost* followed quickly; writers were released in large numbers, not just in Europe but elsewhere, for instance in Vietnam. Von Vegesack found himself running a committee that had its work cut out to keep up with all the many changes occurring across the globe.

However, the period of optimism was short-lived. In 1989, the Tiananmen Square Democracy Movement was brutally stamped out in China; elsewhere, the imprisonment of dissidents continued unabated. And Latin America's habit of simply killing its turbulent priests began to be adopted with alarming frequency in other parts of the world.

Today, the Committee is chaired by the American novelist Joanne Leedom-Ackerman. Post-Cold War, PEN has found that long-term detention persists in some areas (most notably China and Turkey), but elsewhere, censorship has begun to change in nature. The Writers in Prison Committee of PEN is still needed – hundreds of writers and journalists visit their countries' prisons each year for varying lengths of time. But new and frightening forms of censorship have begun to emerge, and the Committee has extended its mandate so as to respond to such problems as death threats and assassinations.

PEN officers are often asked how effective their letters, press releases, demonstrations, petitions and protests are: 'Do you really think the president of X-country is actually going to read, let alone be persuaded by, your letters?' they ask. 'How do you measure effectiveness?' It is a valid query, and there is no easy reply. Perhaps PEN has had most visible results in cases where behind-closed-doors diplomacy was employed. A quiet conversation between an eminent writer and a head of state has, most definitely, resulted in a release here and there. However, PEN has also adopted more public positions, passing resolutions and expressing disapprobation of tyrannical governments in the major newspapers. Does this posturing do any good?

Its effectiveness is dependent on the extent to which a government can be shamed; and this is in turn dependent on the extent to which the international community can build a forum for debate, discussion and co-operativeness where effective 'shaming' can occur. Human rights groups ultimately depend on the functioning of such institutions as the United Nations. And, as the year 2000 approaches, these institutions face greater stresses and trials. Should they prove to be a failed experiment of the twentieth century, then the outlook for human rights protection will be bleak indeed.

Yet, there is another reason why PEN's public posturing is an essential component of its work: whether or not its letters are read, filed away, thrown out or left to collect dust in some basement office of the Ministry of Justice, the letters must still be sent, and must be seen to have been sent. Word of PEN's concern, even if it does not result in an amnesty, usually (if mysteriously) reaches the imprisoned writer in his or her cell. Time and again, PEN has been told by prisoners on their release that, whatever the facts of the matter, *they* attribute their ultimate deliverance, or their improved treatment, to letters such as these. Maybe they are wrong; maybe more complex politics were the true factor. One thing they do not mistake is the support they feel from the attention of the international community. The following letter from the Czech author Eva Kanturkova, sent to the Swedish PEN in 1982, attests this:

> An innocent person suffers in prison feelings of isolation, loneliness, and loss. The knowledge that you defended me against unjust accusations brought me joy and strengthened my will to come to terms with the harsh conditions of my imprisonment.

Simple words: but her affidavit to the worth of PEN's work is sufficient reason for its work to continue.

Prison writing: a genre

Since so many first-rate writers of the twentieth century have found themselves behind bars, it is hardly surprising that the body of work they have produced about their experiences rates the term 'genre'. As stated earlier, this anthology is first a testament to these writers and what they have witnessed: but, second, it is an attempt to explore the genre in a literary sense. The two aims are not usually in competition, as authenticity of the narrator's voice makes for good literature. Very often, the best prison writing does not display a florid style: metaphor, image, language experiment are rarely to be found in the body of prison literature. A plain narration in a simple, unpretentious style is usually favoured, even by those who prefer to write more ornately when they address other subjects. Writers who aim for a more complex or poetic style often run the risk of seeming either precious or insincere. Notable exceptions to this rule are Yannis Ritsos (see 'Broadening') and Wole Soyinka – two of the century's giant literary figures with the genius to carry off a more ambitious approach, even with this difficult subject matter.

Interestingly enough, however, the best prison literature does not always come from the pre-eminent writers who were already skilled at their art before being jailed. Much of it does; but for every celebrated writer who goes to prison and produces there the next book, there is another who finds that the ink has run dry. In fact, some of the best literature (Albie Sachs and Nien Cheng spring to mind) comes from writers who only found their voice while (or even after) being in prison.

Another interesting aspect of the genre is that not all the literature is in the first person. Many writers – for example, Koestler, Nazim Hikmet – prefer the third person at times, as this lends greater objectivity to their tale. The Moroccan writer Abdellatif Laabi uses the second person, thus dragging the reader by the lapel and plunging him into the prison cell.

Not surprisingly, hell is a major theme. It is usually the Greek and Roman concept of hell, Tartarus, that the writers in these pages use. Tartarus is a place where punishment is dovetailed to the individual, so as uniquely to chastise and torment the intended victim. There are at least four references to Tartarus in this book: Vallejo of Peru refers to his warder as 'Cerberus'; Soyinka of Nigeria refers to Tityus, whose hubris condemns him to an eternity of having his liver pecked out by a vulture; Primo Levi, in Auschwitz, refers to Tantalus, whose greed is punished by having a delicious banquet forever just beyond his reach; and Shahrnush Parsipur of Iran refers to Sisyphus, whose punishment for murdering his son was to push up a hill a rock that forever rolled down again. Although there are common deprivations that all prisoners must face (bars, hard floors, primitive sanitation, limited access to anything from the outside world), what seems to terrify these writers most are the deprivations each must face on their own: an interrogation officer whose knowledge of your personal file enables him to taunt you in ways even you could never have dreamed of; constant worry about your spouse, parent or child; an individual fear of pests, darkness, nightmares, or of going mad, self-mutilation and suicide.

The tales of individual horrors and fears reflected in the literature are countless. Just as countless, however, are the descriptions of surmounting them. Survival is a central theme. It is not just physical survival that is at stake: the genre is far more about retaining integrity, in all its senses. Timerman, believing himself on the point of insanity, writes poems after the manner of Stephen Spender. Soyinka fights claustrophobia and panic by means of mantras that include references to dim light sources such as the moon. Commonly, prisoners seize on other life forms such as spiders, mice and mosquitoes in order to retain a connection with reality. They also meditate on the works of other imprisoned writers, searching for the key to remaining integrated. There are many cross-references: Izzat Ghazzawi applauds Nazim Hikmet, Ngugi wa Thiong'o applauds Dennis Brutus, and so on.

One surprising discovery about the genre is that in nearly all cases the ability to transcend prison deprivation does not come from the knowledge that there is a world outside. Hope and release dates have little role to play in prison life. Indeed, prison visits, or sudden longings for the outside world, can cause as much grief as consolation. Survival has a grittier root: stubbornness and refusal to compromise, even where there is nothing to gain, are its hallmarks. Self-interest is an important factor too, a sad fact which in life after prison can cause prisoners much anguish. By and large, anger with the prison lot is used to fuel the will to live and tell the tale. Wanting to tell the tale is another key motivator for the imprisoned writer. Primo Levi's worst nightmare is that he will emerge to tell the tale and nobody will be interested.

In these pages the reader will find less mindless cruelty, suffering and self-aggrandizement than he might have expected. Self-deprecation, humour, love-stories, therapeutic dreams, word games, craftiness, meditation, reflection and friendship are as, or more, common. But, for all the upbeat side of the experience, most readers will agree, once they have read these pages, that prison is indeed a terrible place. Perhaps the most haunting pieces are those in which the writer reflects on where the brutality of the place has its origins. Soyinka and Timerman, and most especially Primo Levi, capture in their work the despair they faced on realizing that the darkness of the prison is in reality an extension of the darkness within themselves; that prison is at once a metaphor for the world, just as Shakespeare's Richard II suggests in his famous Act 5 soliloquy before his murder, but it is also a metaphor for the human spirit in its most vulgar and debased moments.

My choice of title reflects this stark reality: prison is not necessarily a generator of heroes and Nobel laureates. It is ultimately an evil. It debilitates its victims, both as human beings and sometimes as writers. This is the message which these men and women are urgently trying to convey. And this is why PEN has spent so much of its energies fighting prison, at least where it is used to punish free thought.

SIOBHAN DOWD

Editor's Note

In trying to encapsulate the prison experience in this book, I have eschewed regional sections or chronology. Instead I have taken the genre, and presented splices of it to form a single journey.

Journey is the quality that best sums up the prison experience: it is a journey in time, a journey through hell, a journey from day to night and back to day, a journey from confinement to freedom, a journey of moral transformation, and, in societal terms, a journey from tyranny to democracy.

I have chosen to organize this anthology according to this journey: I have tried to present the literature as a seamless whole, a journey through prison, with minimal extraneous detail such as biographies to distract the reader's attention from the progress of the book. Starting with Koestler's brilliant description of the door closing and the first scrutiny of the cell, I have moved through the themes without a break until the moment of release. I initially tried to use categories, but found them false, since many writers embraced several prison themes (for example, time, boredom, light, claustro-phobia) at once. In the end, while obvious themes such as housekeeping, food, transportation, dreams, torture, meditation and correspondence are clustered together, I have generally allowed the mood of one piece to flow into the next. My aim is for the reader to read the book from cover to cover rather than to 'dip' into it. For those who merely want to 'dip', a full contents page is available at the beginning of the book.

After each extract, I give the author's name, the country where he was imprisoned and the period or year of imprisonment which inspired the piece. The dates do *not* refer necessarily to when the piece was written, which was often many years later. Fuller biograph-ical details appear at the back of the book.

The Cell Door Closes

It is a unique sound. A cell door has no handle, either outside or inside. It cannot be shut except by being slammed. It is made of massive steel and concrete, about four inches thick, and every time it falls to there is a resounding crash just as though a shot has been fired. But this report dies away without an echo. Prison sounds are echo-less and bleak.

When the door has been slammed behind him for the first time, the prisoner stands in the middle of the cell and looks round. I fancy that everyone must behave in more or less the same way.

First of all he gives a fleeting look round the walls and takes a mental inventory of all the objects in what is now to be his domain:

the iron bedstead
the wash-basin
the WC
the barred window

His next action is invariably to try to pull himself up by the iron bars of the window and look out. He fails and his suit is covered with white from the plaster on the wall against which he pressed himself. He desists but decides to practice and master the art of pulling himself up by his hands. Indeed, he makes all sorts of laudable resolutions; he will do exercises every morning and learn a foreign language, and he simply won't let his spirit be broken. He dusts his suit and continues his voyage of exploration round his puny realm – five paces long by four paces broad. He tries the iron bedstead. The springs are broken, the wire mattress sags and cuts into the flesh; it's like lying in a hammock made of steel wire. He pulls a face, being determined to prove that he is full of courage and confidence. Then his gaze rests on the cell door, and he sees that an eye is glued to the spy-hole and is watching him.

The eye goggles at him glassily, its pupil unbelievably big. It is an eye without a man attached to it and for a few moments the prisoner's heart stops beating.

The eye disappears and the prisoner takes a deep breath and presses his hand against the left side of his chest.

'Now then,' he says to himself encouragingly, 'how silly to go and get so frightened. You must get used to that. After all the official's only doing his duty by peeping in. That's part of being in prison. But they won't get me down, they'll never get me down. I'll stuff paper in the spy-hole at night . . .'

As a matter of fact there's no reason why he shouldn't do so straight away. The idea fills him with genuine enthusiasm. For the first time he experiences that almost maniac desire for activity that from now on will alternate continually – up and down in a never-ending zig-zag – with melancholia and depression.

Then he realizes that he has no paper on him, and his next impulse is – according to his social status – either to ring or to run over to the stationer's at the corner. This impulse lasts only the fraction of a second. The next moment he becomes conscious for the first time of the true significance of his situation. For the first time he grasps the full reality of being behind a door which is locked from outside, grasps it in all its searing, devastating poignancy. . . .

And this is how things are to go on – in the coming minutes, hours, days, weeks, years.

How long has he already been in the cell?

He looks at his watch: exactly three minutes.

ARTHUR KOESTLER, Spain, 1937
(from *Dialogue with Death*)

Cerberus

Cerberus four times
a day wields his padlock, opening
closing our breastbones, with winks
we understand perfectly.

With his sad, baggy-assed pants,
boyish in transcendental scruffiness,
standing up, the poor old man is adorable.
He jokes with the prisoners, their groins
brimming with their fists. And even jolly
he gnaws some crust for them; but always
doing his duty.

In between the bars he pokes the fiscal
point, unnoticed, hoisting on the third phalanx
of his little finger,
on the trail of what I say,
what I eat,
what I dream.
This raven doesn't want any inwardness,
and how much pain for us is in what Cerberus wants.

Through a clockwork system, the imminent,
Pythagorean! old man plays
widthwise in our aortas. And solely

from time to night, at night
he somewhat shirks his exception from metal.
But, naturally,
always doing his duty.

CESAR VALLEJO, Peru, 1921
(translated by Clayton Eshleman)

Colesberg:
En Route to Robben Island

Cold

the clammy cement
sucks our naked feet

a rheumy yellow bulb
lights a damp grey wall

the stubbled grass
wet with three o'clock dew
is black with glittery edges;

we sit on the concrete,
stuff with our fingers
the sugarless pap
into our mouths

then labour erect;

form lines;

steel ourselves into fortitude
or accept an image of ourselves
numb with resigned acceptance;

the grizzled senior warder comments:
'Things like these
I have no time for;

they are worse than rats;
you can only shoot them.'

Overhead
the large frosty glitter of the stars
the Southern Cross flowering low;

the chains on our ankles
and wrists
that pair us together
jangle

glitter.

We begin to move
  awkwardly.

DENNIS BRUTUS, South Africa, *c.* 1963
(from *A Simple Lust*, 1973)

Housekeeping

As I followed the female guard, I breathed deeply the sweet night air. We walked around the main building, passed through a peeling and faded red gate with a feeble light, and entered a smaller courtyard where I saw a two-storey structure. This was where the women prisoners were housed.

From a room near the entrance, another female guard emerged yawning. I was handed over to her in silence.

'Come along,' she said sleepily, leading me through a passage lined with bolted, heavily padlocked doors. My first sight of the prison corridor was something I have never been able to forget. In subsequent years, in my dreams and nightmares, I saw it again and again, in the dim light, the long line of doors with sinister-looking bolts and padlocks outside, and felt again and again the helplessness and frustration of being locked inside.

When we reached the end of the corridor, the guard unlocked a door on the left to reveal an empty cell.

'Get in,' she said. 'Have you any belongings?'

I shook my head.

'We'll notify your family in the morning and get them to send you your belongings. Now go to sleep!'

I asked her whether I could go to the toilet. She pointed to a cement fixture in the left-hand corner of the room and said, 'I'll lend you some toilet paper.'

She pushed the bolt in place with a loud clang and locked the door. I heard her moving away down the corridor.

I looked around the room, and my heart sank. Cobwebs dangled from the ceiling; the once whitewashed walls were yellow with age and streaked with dust. The single bulb was coated with grime and extremely dim. Patches of the cement floor were black with dampness. A strong musty smell pervaded the air. I hastened to open the only small window, with its rust-pitted iron bars. To reach it, I had to stand on tiptoe. When I succeeded in pulling the knob and the window swung open, flakes of peeling paint as well as a shower of dust fell to the floor. The only furniture in the room was three narrow beds of rough wooden planks, one against the wall, the other two stacked one on top of the other. Never in my life had I been in or even imagined a place so primitive and filthy.

The guard came back with several sheets of toilet paper of the roughest kind, which she handed to me through a small square window in the door of the cell, saying, 'There you are! When you get your supply, you must return to the government the same number of sheets. Now go to sleep. Lie with your head towards the door. That's the regulation.'

I could not bring myself to touch the dust-covered bed. But I needed to lie down, as my legs were badly swollen. I pulled the bed away from the dirty wall and wiped it with the toilet paper. But the dirt was so deeply ingrained that I could only remove the loose dust. Then I lay down anyhow and closed my eyes. The naked bulb hanging from the center of the ceiling was directly about my head. Though dim, it irritated me. I looked around the cell but could not see a light switch anywhere.

'Please, excuse me!' I called, knocking on the door with my hand.

'Quiet, quiet!' The guard hurried over and slid open the shutter on the small window.

'I can't find the light switch,' I told her.

'We don't switch off the light at night here. In future, when you want to speak to the guards, just say, "Report." Don't knock on the door. Don't say anything else.'

'Could you lend me a broom to sweep the room? It's so dirty.'

'What nonsense! It's past two o'clock. You just go to sleep!'

She closed the shutter but remained outside and watched me through the peephole to make sure I obeyed her orders.

I lay down on the bed again and turned to face the dusty wall to avoid the light. I closed my eyes to shut out the sight of the wall, but I had to inhale the unpleasant smell of dampness and dust that surrounded me. In the distance, I heard faintly the crescendo of noise from the crowds on the streets.

The next day
The dirt in the cell was intolerable. I simply had to deal with it if I was going to live in that cell for another night. Besides, I had always found physical work soothing for frayed nerves. I asked the guard whether I could borrow a broom to sweep the floor.

'You are allowed to borrow a broom on Sundays only. But since you have just come, I'll lend you one today.'

A few moments later she came back with an old, worn broom, which she squeezed through the small window to me. I pulled the bed around the cell and stood on it to reach the cobwebs. When I brushed the walls, the cell was enveloped in a cloud of dust.

The shutter opened again. A sheet of paper was pushed through to me. Looking out, I saw a male guard standing there.

'The money you brought here last night has been banked for you. This is your receipt. You are allowed to use the money to buy daily necessities such as toilet paper, soap, and towels,' he said.

'That's just what I need. Could I buy some now?' I asked him.

'You may buy what you need,' the man said.

'Please get me a washbasin, two enameled mugs for eating and drinking, some sewing thread, needles, soap, towels, a toothbrush and toothpaste, and some toilet paper. Am I allowed to buy some cold cream?'

'No, only necessities.'

Soon he returned with a washbasin decorated with two large roses, six towels with colorful stripes, a stack of toilet paper, six cakes of the cheapest kind of laundry soap, two enameled mugs with lids, a toothbrush, a tube of toothpaste, and two spools of coarse cotton thread. He told me the prisoners were not allowed to have needles in the cell but they could borrow them from the guards on Sundays.

The guard had to open the cell door to hand me the washbasin. While it was still open, another male guard brought me the clothes and bedding left me by the Red Guards, as well as *The Collected Works of Mao Zedong* and the Little Red Book of Mao's quotations. After I had signed the receipt for these things, the two guards locked the door and departed. . . .

I decided to tackle the dirty room. What I needed was some water.

'Report!' I went to the door and called.

It was another female guard who pushed open the shutter and said sternly, 'You don't have to shout! Now what do you want?'

I knew from her tone of voice that she would probably refuse whatever I might request. To forestall such a possibility, I quickly recited a quotation of Mao that said, 'To be hygienic is glorious; to be unhygienic is a shame.' Then I asked, 'May I have some water to clean the cell?'

20

She walked away without saying a word. I waited and waited. Eventually the Labor Reform girl came and gave me enough water to fill the new washbasin as well as the one brought from my home with my things. First I washed the bed thoroughly; then I climbed onto my rolled-up bedding to wipe the dust-smeared windowpanes so that more light could come into the room. After I had washed the cement toilet built into the corner of the cell, I still had enough cold water left to bathe myself and rinse out my dirty blouse. When hot water for drinking was issued, I sat on the clean bed and drank it with enjoyment. Plain boiled water had never tasted so good.

NIEN CHENG, China, 1967–1973
(from *Life and Death in Shanghai*, 1986)

Scrubbing the Furious Walls of Mikuyu

Is this where they dump those rebels,
these haggard cells stinking of bucket
shit and vomit and the acrid urine of
yesteryears? Who would have thought I
would be gazing at these dusty, cobweb
ceilings of Mikuyu Prison, scrubbing
briny walls and riddling out impetuous
scratches of another dung-beetle locked
up before me here? Violent human palms
wounded these blood-bloated mosquitoes
and bugs (to survive), leaving these vicious
red marks. Monstrous flying cockroaches
crashed here. Up there the cobwebs trapped
dead bumblebees. Where did black wasps
get clay to build nests in this corner?

But here, scratches, insolent scratches!
I have marvelled at the rock paintings
of Mphunzi Hills once but these grooves
and notches on the walls of Mikuyu Prison,
how furious, what barbarous squiggles!
How long did this anger languish without
charge or trial without visit here and
what justice committed? This is the moment
we dreaded; when we'd all descend into
the pit, alone; without a wife or a child
without mother; without paper or pencil
without a story (just three Bibles for
ninety men) without charge without trial.
This is the moment I never needed to see.

Shall I scrub these brave squiggles out
of human memory then or should I perhaps

superimpose my own, less caustic; dare I
overwrite this precious scrawl? Who'd
have known I'd find another prey without
charge without trial (without bitterness)
in these otherwise blank walls of Mikuyu
Prison? No, I will throw my water and mop
elsewhere. We have liquidated too many
brave names out of the nation's memory;
I will not rub out another nor inscribe
my own, more ignoble, to consummate this
moment of truth I have always feared.

JACK MAPANJE, Malawi, *c.* 1987
(from *The Chattering Wagtails of Mikuyu Prison*, 1993)

Throwing Time into Tins

We have learned, indeed, to throw time into tins
And have stirred in the condensed night at all times.
This century grows ever darker, and the next will not come soon,
To wipe clean the names off yesterday's prison wall.

We loaded it with the voices of departing friends,
With the names of unborn children – for a new wall.
We equipped it so lovingly, but we ourselves
Do not row in it, we are not even allowed on board.

But covering the measured-out load with coarse matting
We still manage to broadcast the seed.
Our hands are torn but we still pluck out the dragon's
Teeth from the crops, which are fated to stand after us.

IRINA RATUSHINSKAYA, former USSR, 1982–1986
(from *Pencil Letter*, 1988; translated by Richard McKane
with Helen Szamuely)

First Cell, First Love

How is one to take the title of this chapter? A cell and love in the same breath? . . .

You sit down and half-close your eyes and try to remember them all. How many different cells you were imprisoned in during your term! It is difficult to count them. And in each one there were people, people. There might be two people in one, 150 in another. You were imprisoned for five minutes in one and all summer long in another.

But in every case, out of all the cells you've been in, your first cell is a very special one, the place where you first encountered others like yourself, doomed to the same fate. All your life you will remember it with an emotion that you otherwise experience only in remembering your first love. And those people, who shared with you the floor and air of that stone cubicle during those days when you rethought your entire life, will from time to time be recollected by you as members of your own family. Yes, in those days they *were* your only family.

What you experience in your first interrogation cell parallels nothing in your entire previous life or your whole subsequent life. No doubt prisons have stood for thousands of years before you came along, and may continue to stand after you too – longer than one would like to think – but that first interrogation cell is unique and inimitable.

Maybe it was a terrible place for a human being. A lice-laden, bug-infested lock-up, without windows, without ventilation, without bunks, and with a dirty floor. . . . Or maybe it was a 'solitary' in the Archangel prison, where the glass had been smeared over with red lead so that the only rays of God's maimed light which crept into you were crimson, and where a 15-watt bulb burned constantly in the ceiling, day and night. Or a 'solitary' in the city of Choibalsan, where, for six months at a time, fourteen of you were crowded onto seven square yards of floor space in such a way that you could only shift your bent legs in unison. Or it was one of the Lefortovo 'psychological' cells, like No.111, which was painted black and also had a day-and-night 25-watt bulb, but was in all other respects like every other Lefortovo cell: asphalt floor; the heating valve out in the corridor where only the guards had access to it; and above all, that interminable irritating roar from the wind tunnel of the neighboring Central Aero- and Hydrodynamics Institute – a roar one could not believe was unintentional, a roar which would make a bowl or cup vibrate so violently that it would slip off the edge of the table, a roar which made it useless to converse and during which one could sing at the top of one's lungs and the jailer wouldn't ever hear. And then when the roar stopped, there would ensue a sense of relief or felicity superior to freedom itself.

But it was not the dirty floor, not the murky walls, nor the odor of the latrine bucket that you loved – but those fellow prisoners with whom you about-faced at command, that something which beat between your heart and theirs, their sometimes astonishing words, and then, too, the birth within you, on that very spot, of free-floating thought.

ALEXANDER SOLZHENITSYN, former USSR, 1945–1953
(from *The Gulag Archipelago*, 1973)

The Eye

Tonight, a guard, not following the rules, leaves the peephole ajar. I wait a while to see what will happen but it remains open. Standing on tiptoe, I peer out. There's a narrow corridor, and across from my cell I can see at least two other doors. Indeed, I have a full view of two doors. What a sensation of freedom! An entire universe added to my Time, that elongated time which hovers over me oppressively in the cell. Time, that dangerous enemy of man, when its existence, duration and eternity are virtually palpable.

The light in the corridor is strong. Momentarily blinded, I step back, then hungrily return. I try to fill myself with the visible space. So long have I been deprived of a sense of distance and proportion that I feel suddenly unleashed. In order to look out, I must lean my face against the icy steel door. As the minutes pass, the cold becomes unbearable. My entire forehead is pressed against the steel and the cold makes my head ache. But it's been a long time – how long? – without a celebration of space. I press my ear against the door, yet hear no sound. I resume looking.

He is doing the same. I suddenly realize that the peephole in the door facing mine is also open and that there's an eye behind it. I'm startled: They've laid a trap for me. Looking through the peephole is forbidden and they've seen me doing it. I step back and wait. I wait for some Time, more Time, and again more Time. And then return to the peephole.

He is doing the same.

And now I must talk about you, about that long night we spent together, during which you were my brother, my father, my son, my friend. Or, are you a woman? If so, we passed that night as lovers. You were merely an eye, yet you too remember that night, don't you? Later I was told you had died, that you had a weak heart and couldn't survive the 'machine', but they didn't mention whether you were a man or a woman. How can you have died, considering that night we conquered death?

You must remember, I need you to remember, for otherwise I'm obliged to remember for us both, and the beauty we experienced requires your testimony as well. You blinked. I clearly recall you blinking. And that flutter of movement proved conclusively that I was not the last human survivor on earth amid this universe of torturing custodians. At times, inside my cell, I'd move an arm or a leg merely to view a movement that was nonviolent, that differed from the ones employed when I was dragged or pushed by the guards. And you blinked. It was beautiful.

You were – you are? – a person of high human qualities, endowed certainly with a profound knowledge of life, for you invented all sorts of games that night, creating Movement in our confined world. You'd suddenly move away, then return. At first I was frightened. But then I realized you were recreating the great human adventure of lost-and-found and I played the game with you. Sometimes we'd return to the peephole at the same time, and our sense of triumph was so powerful we felt immortal. We were immortal.

I was frightened a second time when you disappeared for a long interval. Desperately I pressed against the peephole, my forehead frozen on that cold night – it was night, wasn't it? – and I took off my shirt and propped it under my forehead. When you returned I was furious, and you undoubtedly saw my fury for you didn't disappear again. This must have been a great effort for you. A few days later, when taken for a session with the 'machine', I heard one guard comment to another about his having used your crutches for kindling. I'm sure that you're aware, though, that such ruses were often used to soften up a prisoner before a 'machine' session – a chat with Susan, as they called it. And I didn't believe them. I swear to you I didn't believe them. No one could destroy for me the mutual immortality created during that night of love and comradeship.

You were – you are? – extremely intelligent. Only one possible outgoing act would have occurred to me: looking out, looking, ceaselessly looking. But you unexpectedly stuck your chin in front of the peephole. Then your mouth, or part of your forehead. I was desperate. And frightened. I remained glued to the peephole, but only in order to peer out of it. I tried, I assure you, even briefly, to put my cheek to the opening, whereupon the inside of my cell sprang into view and my spirits immediately dropped. The gap between life and solitude was so evident; knowing that you were nearby, I couldn't bear gazing back toward my cell. You forgave me for this, retaining your vitality and mobility. I realized that you were consoling me, and I started to cry. In silence, of course. You needn't worry. I knew that I couldn't risk uttering a sound. You saw me crying, though, didn't you? You did see that. It did me good, crying in front of you. You know how dismal it is to be in a cell and to say to yourself, It's time to cry a bit, whereupon you cry hoarsely, wretchedly, heedlessly. With you I was able to cry serenely, peacefully, as if allowed to cry. As if everything might be poured into that sobbing, converting it into a prayer rather than tears. You can't imagine how I detested that fitful sobbing of mine inside the cell. That night, you taught me how we could be comrades-in-tears.

I don't know why, but I'm sure that you are – that you were? – a young man of medium height. Let's say thirty-five years old, with a great sense of humor. A few days later a guard came to my cell to soften me up. He gave me a cigarette: it was his turn to play the good guy. He advised me to spill everything, told me that he'd had plenty of experience and that a person my age winds up dying in Susan's arms because his heart can't withstand the electric shocks for long. And he informed me that you'd been 'cooled out'. This is how he put it: 'Look, Jacobo, the only obligation you have is to survive. Politics change. . . . You have children. In the cell facing yours there was a crazy guy. We cooled him out. Look, Jacobo. . . .'

I didn't believe him. If I was able to withstand it, certainly you were. Did you have a weak heart? Impossible. You were strong-hearted, generous, brave. Such hearts are not destroyed by Susan. Do you remember once how the lights went off? Do you know what I did? I sat down on the mattress, wrapped myself in the blanket, and pretended to sleep. I was very frightened. Suddenly I realized that I hadn't put on my shirt. I did so hastily. But the lights went on again. And I remembered that the guards sometimes amused themselves by turning the lights off and on. It's possible, of course, that a large amount of current was being consumed by Susan. Undoubtedly, several new prisoners had arrived, and the first thing automatically done to them was to put them through the machine, even before they were asked who they were. The prisoner's first sensation had to be a session of electric shocks in order to lower his defenses on admittance. I found out later that this technique was changed after some individuals were cooled out before they could even be questioned. Not even the doctor on duty (by the way, do you remember how that doctor kept letting his beard grow, then after a few weeks would shave it off, then let his mustache grow, then only his sideburns, then he'd wear his hair long, then short, all because he was so scared of being identified?) no, not even the doctor was always able to save them.

Yet both of us survived. Do you remember when I got a cramp in my leg while they were torturing me and suddenly my outcries ceased? They thought I had 'gone', and were alarmed. They had orders to get me to confess because they wanted to build a big case around me. I wasn't any use to them dead. Yes, I was paralysed for a moment due to the cramp. It's curious how one can experience pain and joy simultaneously. Although my eyes were blindfolded, I sensed their fear – and rejoiced. Then I began moaning again on account of Susan.

No, I don't think you remember this, though I tried to tell you about it. Yet your eye was much more expressive than mine. I tried to convey the episode to you, for it was as if a battle had been won against them. But at that point I was terribly confused, and it's possible that I meant to tell it to you without actually having done so.

My friend, my brother, how much I learned that night from you. According to my calculations, it must have been April or May 1977. Suddenly you put your nose in front of the peephole and rubbed it. It was a caress, wasn't it? Yes, a caress. You'd already incorporated so many levels of experience into our captivity, yet persisted in the restoration of our humanity. At that moment you were suggesting tenderness, caressing your nose, gazing at me. You repeated it several times. A caress, then your eye. Another caress, and your eye. You may have thought I didn't understand. But we understood each other from the start. I knew clearly you were telling me that tenderness would reappear. I don't know why you felt the urgency that night to affirm the equal importance, or even greater importance, of tenderness over love. Is it because tenderness contains an element of resignation, and perhaps that night you were feeling resigned? Is it because tenderness is consoling to someone already resigned? Tenderness is indeed a consolation, whereas love is a need. And you assuredly needed to be consoled. I didn't understand that, but you, my brother, my friend, my comrade-in-tears, were you already aware of this and resigned to it? If so, why and for whom am I uttering all these inanities? Am I babbling to myself like a fool? Is there really no eye gazing at me?

JACOBO TIMERMAN, Argentina, 1977
(from *Prisoner without a Name, Cell without a Number*, 1981, translated by Toby Talbot)

Erasmus and Mosquitoes

One of the very few things I have been able to keep here is a picture of Erasmus. It's a newspaper clipping. I cut it sometime ago and now I often look at it. It gives me a certain sense of peace. I suppose there must be some explanation for this, but I'm not interested in explanations. It is enough that there is this magic, this strange exaltation caused by the identification of this man with our own values, this victory over my solitude, which started centuries ago and which becomes real again as I look at his face. He is shown in profile. I like that. He is not looking at me, but he is telling me where to look. He reveals a solidarity of vision between us. In prison, this solidarity is a daily necessity, like the need for water, bread, sleep. When they search my cell they come upon Erasmus' picture, but they let me keep it. They don't understand. They've no idea how dangerous a mild, wise man can be. Sometimes I wonder about the jailer's eye, watching me through the hole in the door – where does he find solidarity of vision?

I would like to write about another friendship I formed the autumn before last. I think it has some significance. It shows the solidarity that can be forged between unhappy creatures. I had been kept in solitary confinement for four months. I hadn't seen a soul throughout that period. Only uniforms – inquisitors and jailers. One day, I noticed three mosquitoes in my cell. They were struggling hard to resist the cold that was just beginning. In the daytime they slept on the wall. At night they would come buzzing over to me. In the beginning, they exasperated me. But fortunately I soon understood that I too was struggling hard to live through the cold spell. What were they asking me? Something unimportant. A drop of blood – it would save them. I couldn't refuse. At nightfall I would bare my arm and wait for them. After some days they got used to me and they were no longer afraid. They would come to me quite naturally, openly. This trust is something I owe them. Thanks to them, the world was no longer merely an inquisition chamber. Then one day I was transferred to another prison. I never saw my mosquitoes again. This is how you are deprived of the presence of your friends in the arbitrary world of prisons. But you go on thinking of them often.

During the months when I was being interrogated, alone before those men with the multiple eyes of a spider – and the instincts of a spider – one night a policeman on guard smiled at me. At that moment, the policeman was all men to me. Four months later, when the representative of the International Red Cross walked into my cell, once again I saw all men in his friendly face.

When one day they finally put me in a cell with another prisoner and he began to talk to me about the thing he loved most in life – sailing and fishing boats – this man too was all men to me. It is true, then, that there are situations in which each one of us represents all mankind.

And it is the same with these papers: I have entrusted them to a poor Italian prisoner who has just been released and who was willing to try and smuggle them out for me. Through him I hope they will eventually reach you. That man is all men to me.

But I think it is time I finished. We over here in prison, and you out there who agree with us. Freedom: my love.

GEORGE MANGAKIS, Greece, *c.* 1970
(from *Letter to the Europeans*)

The Spider

Within the gloomy cell, I studied Mao's books many hours a day, reading until my eyesight became blurred.

One day, in the early afternoon, when my eyes were too tired to distinguish the printed words, I lifted them from the book to gaze at the window. A small spider crawled into view, climbing up one of the rust-eroded bars. The little creature was no bigger than a good-sized pea; I would not have seen it if the wooden frame nailed to the wall outside to cover the lower half of the window hadn't been painted black. I watched it crawl slowly but steadily to the top of the iron bar, quite a long walk for such a tiny thing, I thought. When it reached the top, suddenly it swung out and descended on a thin silken thread spun from one end of its body. With a leap and swing, it secured the end of the thread to another bar. The spider then crawled back along the silken thread to where it had started and swung out in another direction on a similar thread. I watched the tiny creature at work with increasing fascination. It seemed to know exactly what to do and where to take the next thread. There was no hesitation, no mistake, and no haste. It knew its job and was carrying it out with confidence. When the frame was made, the spider proceeded to weave a web that was intricately beautiful and absolutely perfect, with all the strands of thread evenly spaced. When the web was completed, the spider went to its center and settled there.

I had just watched an architectural feat by an extremely skilled artist, and my mind was full of questions. Who had taught the spider to make a web? Could it really have acquired the skill through evolution or did God create the spider and endow it with the ability to make a web so that it could catch food and perpetuate its species? How big was the brain of such a tiny creature? Did it act simply by instinct, or had it somehow learned to store the knowledge of web-making? Perhaps one day I would ask an entomologist. For the moment, I knew I had just witnessed something that was extraordinarily beautiful and uplifting. . . .

My cell faced southwest. For a brief moment, the rays of the setting sun turned the newly made web into a glittering disc of rainbow colors, before it shifted further west and sank below the horizon. I did not dare to go up to the window in case I should frighten the spider away. I remained where I was, watching it. I soon discovered it was not merely sitting there waiting for its prey but was forever vigilant. Whenever a corner of the web was ruffled or torn by the breeze, the spider was there in an instant to repair the damage. And as days passed, the spider renewed the web from time to time; sometimes a part of it was remade, sometimes the whole web was remade.

I became very attached to the little creature after watching its activities and gaining an understanding of its habits. First thing in the morning, throughout the day, and last thing at night, I would look at it and feel reassured when I saw that it was still there. The tiny spider became my companion. My spirits lightened. The depressing feeling of complete isolation was broken by having another living thing near me, even though it was so tiny and incapable of response.

Soon it was November. The wind shifted to the northwest. With each rainy day the temperature fell further. I watched the spider anxiously, not wishing to close the window and shut it out. It went on repairing the wind-torn web and patiently making new ones. However, one morning, when I woke up, I found the spider gone. Its derelict web was in shreds. I felt sad but hopefully kept the window open in case it should come back. Then I chanced to look up and saw my small friend sitting in the center of a newly made web in a corner of the ceiling. I quickly closed the window, happy to know that my friend had not deserted me.

NIEN CHENG, China, 1967–1973
(from *Life and Death in Shanghai*, 1986)

Sins of the Father

To you and my beloved children,

Now winter seems to be approaching, step-by-step. I am already worried because it is said this coming winter is very likely to be the severest in this century. The twenty-fifth was one day after the first frost, and the temperature dipped quite a bit.

It was heartbreaking when I went out to the flower beds and saw that all the flowers except the chrysanthemums had vanished. Petunias, globe amaranths, hollyhocks, yellow cosmos, and cockscomb – I grew them with all the care I could give and kept them going for more than a month longer than the ones in the other flower beds. One good frost, and they were gone in a morning. When I saw the miserable shapes of the flowers, I was overcome by feelings of sadness and emptiness, as if I were watching a loved one on a deathbed. Human beings are bound to be attracted to something, and once attracted, they have to taste the sorrow of parting sometime. This is what I felt all over again.

As I briefly mentioned yesterday during the visit, I had a severe case of indigestion from the night of the 22nd and was in great pain for two or three days. I was groaning in pain because the front and back of my chest felt as if they were pulling each other. . . . While I was ailing I got so homesick I was constantly thinking that all I wanted was you at my side, taking care of me. Lying on my bed, with a needle in my arm for the injection of Ringer's solution, I spent the hours of boredom in sundry thoughts about my life, asking myself questions, then answering them.

- And what is this called my life? Throughout my life there has been one adversity after another, and I have reached this age without once having lived happily – free of all worry, with my family – like other people. Can we still say that this is living?

- This does not mean, however, that living comfortably is the only road to happiness, does it? Among the people we know who live such lives, how many are there who can confidently say they have been happy? When they reflect on life, they will regret that they have spent their lives meaninglessly, in pursuit of comfort.

- Nonetheless, this is also a matter of degree. If one's life is spent in poverty and pain and in a continuum of death and adversity, such as mine has been, how can one not doubt the meaning of life?

- Does this mean, then, that I am having second thoughts about the life I have lived? Do I regret the life that I have tried to live sincerely for my people and conscience, the life that tries not to bequeath to posterity the sorrowful times we have endured?

- I am not going to say I have second thoughts. As Hong-up said some time ago, however, it is too much to say that I alone must live this kind of ordeal. Furthermore, it has not been only my personal ordeal. My family and so many of my brothers, relatives and friends have been sacrificed because of me. I cannot describe how my heart aches whenever I think about them. There is nothing in this world more anguishing than idly watching other people suffer on my account. . . .

- Actually, we frequently become skeptical about the meaning of life. After all, what does adversity mean? Is it a punishment for one's sin? If so, how is it that we observe innumerable instances of bad people prospering while good ones are crushed?

  Si Maxian, who may be considered the father of history, at least in the Orient, raised the issue of 'a way of heaven' formally in his historical biographies. He earned the ire of the Han dynasty's Mu emperor when he presented a justifiable defense for a friend. For this he was castrated, which for a man is worse punishment than dying. When we think of him as exemplary of a good man suffering, his outcry over whether there is or is not a way of heaven affects us even more deeply.

- I have given this problem a lot of thought. Actually, why good men suffer and bad ones prosper is a long-standing puzzle; indeed, it has not been solved in the history of human religion and ethics. What is clear, however, is that this problem can never be solved using the logic that adversity is a punishment, whereas success is a reward for good deeds. One opinion [that may be useful here] was advanced by Dostoevsky. In *Brothers Karamazov*, Dmitri Karamazov received a guilty verdict he did not deserve after being falsely accused of having murdered his father. He came to a certain understanding at that time by overcoming many psychological conflicts, anguish, and anger.

Dmitri's perception was: I do not deserve this. Why, then, do I have to suffer the ordeal of being exiled to Siberia? I am shouldering my countless sins of the past, all sorts of vulgar sins of my father, and the sin of the Russian people. A human being's adversity cannot, and should not, be avoided because as a member of a group, it stems not only from one's own sins but also from the sins of those who make up the community. Thus, he gladly endures the guilty verdict when he realizes its meaning, and it is because of this realization that he is saved.

KIM DAE-JUNG, South Korea, 1985
(from *Prison Writings*, 1987)

Punishment

In this place there is a maze of prisons
and in each prison a myriad of dungeons
and in each dungeon countless cells
and in each cell scores of fettered men.

One amongst these men,
persuaded of his wife's infidelity
plunged his dagger deep.

Another amongst these men,
desperate to put bread in his children's mouths,
slaughtered in the searing summer midday heat.

Some amongst these men
on a quiet rainy day
ambushed the money lender.

Others, in the hush of the alleyway
crept stealthily onto the rooves.
Still others
plundered gold teeth from fresh graves
at midnight.

But I, I have never murdered on a dark and stormy night.
But I, I have never ambushed the money lender.
But I, I have never crept stealthily onto the rooves.

In this place there is a maze of prisons
and in each prison a myriad of dungeons
and in each dungeon countless cells
and in each cell scores of fettered men.

But I, deep in my reveries,
never lend an ear to them. No,
I listen out instead for a dim echo
of the endless song of the desert grass
as it sprouts, shrivels, withers,
scattering to the winds.

And I, were I not a fettered man,
one day at dawn,
like a dim, almost buried, memory,
I would leave this cold, contemptible place.

And this,
This is my crime.

AHMAD SHAMLOO, Iran, *c.* 1959
(translated by Ahmad Ebrahimi and Karina Zabihi)

And Night Fell

On the 16th, the sun rose in a halo of glory. I felt as if I were the only man in the universe waiting for it, and through the window of the ten-by-twelve-paces cell, I saw its rays. It promised to touch the window of my confinement as it played in the ten-by-twenty ceilingless courtyard outside the cell. It did not matter that I was not allowed out of the cell, as long as the sun could kiss the window momentarily and perhaps my face and hands, through the iron bars, the only exposed parts of me.

As it rose higher, I realized its rays slanted southward, touching the entire south wall, signalling its move towards me. By midday, it began to dance away from me, its rays receding eastward on its journey westward, taking a course north of the cell. At about two in the afternoon I had given up hope. Its light was south-east, nowhere near where I was. Towards five o'clock, I saw the shadows made by my cell rising upwards on the east wall, by which time the sun was behind me, growing weaker, about to set. A lonely bird in the nearby park sang its farewell to day, to sun, to man and life and to me, as it went: *Phez'ko mthwal', Phez'ko mthwal', Phez'ko mthwal'.*

I remembered hearing this bird in Vendaland, in the northern Transvaal during my music research projects, and I was to hear it too in Mozambique and in Swaziland, where I went to rest after prison. Khosi Noge, my hostess, explained the lyrics of the bird-tune to me. *Phez'ko mthwal'* meant 'up and onto your burden'.

I sank on the mat, spread out three grey blankets, folded my black jersey to make an uncomfortable pillow and prepared myself to sleep at 5.30 in the afternoon. . . . And, in a little while, night fell.

MOLEFE PHETO, South Africa, 1975
(from *And Night Fell*, 1983)

Seasons and Storms

It is 25 November 1975, when I am sentenced. I shall not be seeing the stars again for many years. In the beginning I don't realize this, I don't miss them. And then suddenly it becomes very important, like chafing sores in the mind – something you've taken for granted for so long and that you now miss, the way you'd miss a burial site if you died in space. It is not natural never to see stars, or the moon for that matter – it is as cruel as depriving people of sound. I see the moon again for the first time on 19 April 1976 when, at about twenty-three minutes to four in the afternoon, I am in the largest of the three exercise yards, which has towering walls, making it rather like a well. I looked up and to my astonishment saw in a patch of sky above a shrivelled white shape. Could it be a pearl in my eye? Was it the afterbirth of a spaceship? No, it could only be the moon. And they told me that she'd been hanged, that she was dead!

The sun and its absence become the pivot of your daily existence. You wait. You build your day around the half hour when you'll be allowed out in the courtyard to say good morning to the sun. You follow its course through the universe behind your eyelids. You become its disciple. The sun knows not of the justice of man. You know exactly where it touches at what time – winter, autumn, or summer – and if you are lucky, as I was for some time, to be kept in a cell just off the main corridor with windows giving onto the catwalk which was not closed to the outside, you would have a glimmer, a suspicion, a hair-crack of sunshine coming in during certain seasons, but never reaching far enough down for you to feel it. I used to climb on my bed, stand on my toes on the bedstead, and then, sometimes, for something like two minutes a day, a yellow wand would brush the top of my hair. Of course, you develop an intense awareness, like a hitherto unexplored sense in yourself, for knowing exactly when the sun rises and when it sets without ever seeing it.

With the first shivers of the very early morning, even before the call for waking up sounded, I used to get out of bed and try to position myself in that one spot of the cell where the warder could not see me directly and then for half an hour sit in *zazen*, and I could always feel in me a very profound source of light inexorably un-nighting the outside: with eyes half closed I could feel it first tipping rose the roof made of glassfiber, giving shape to the trees one knew must be growing not far off, because the birds talked about these trees, and then jumping over the walls which were made of red brick, and generally investing the day. It was the quiet moment then: the *boere* for the morning shift hadn't arrived yet to come and stamp their feet, and those who'd been on for the second watch from twelve at night were nearing the end of their turn of duty and so they were sleepy, perhaps dozing with their rifles in their hands hanging limply.

On summer days when you were cleaning your corridor you could see through the grill clouds passing along the blue highway above the yard wall facing you: boats on their way to a dream, bit actors always dressed in white being taken to an empty space where Fellini would be filming a saturnalia, a wedding feast. There was wind which you never felt on your face but which you got to know through its aftermath – the red Transvaal dust you had to sweep up. There were the most impressive summer thunderstorms tearing and rolling for miles through the ether, slashing and slaying before big-rain came to lash the roof with a million whips. It was like living underneath a gigantic billiard table. Behind the walls with no apertures to the outside, behind the screen of your closed eyes where you hid from the *boere* – you still saw the stabs and the snakes of lightning.

BREYTEN BREYTENBACH, South Africa, *c.* 1975
(from *A Memory of Sky*)

On the Island

1
Cement-grey floors and walls
cement-grey days
cement-grey time
and a grey susurration
as of seas breaking
winds blowing
and rains drizzling

A barred existence
so that one did not need to look
at doors or windows
to know that they were sundered by bars
and one locked in a grey gelid stream
of unmoving time.

2
When the rain came
it came in a quick moving squall
moving across the island
murmuring from afar
then drumming on the roof
then marching fading away.

And sometimes one mistook
the weary tramp of feet
as the men came shuffling from the quarry
white-dust-filmed and shambling
for the rain
that came and drummed and marched away.

3

It was not quite envy
nor impatience
nor irritation
but a mixture of feelings
one felt
for the aloof deep-green dreaming firs
that poised in the island air
withdrawn, composed and still.

4

On Saturday afternoons we were embalmed in time
like specimen moths pressed under glass;
we were immobile in the sunlit afternoon
waiting;
Visiting time:
until suddenly like a book snapped shut
all possibilities vanished as zero hour passed
and we knew another week would have to pass.

DENNIS BRUTUS, South Africa, *c.* 1964
(from *A Simple Lust*, 1973)

A Stitch in Time

I was in Pretoria Central Prison for twenty-eight days. It was like being sealed in a sterile tank of glass in a defunct aquarium. People came to look at me every now and then and left a ration of food. I could see out of my glass case and the view was sharp and clear, but I could establish no identity with what I could see outside, no reciprocal relationship with anyone who hove in view. In [my previous jail] Marshall Square my sooty surroundings and the general air of gloom about the old police station would have justified melancholy, but I had been buoyant and refractory. Pretoria shone of bright polished steel and I grew increasingly subdued. My imprisonment was an abandonment in protracted time. I reflected on the new-found skill of the Security Branch in subjecting people to an enforced separation, a dissociation, from humanity. I felt alien and excluded from the little activity I saw about me; I was bereft of human contact and exchange. What was going on in the outside world? No echoes reached me. I was suspended in limbo, unknowing, unreached.

I read the Bible, day-dreamed, tried to shake myself into disciplined thinking. I devised a plot for a novel. The characters were me and my friends, all cast in heroic mould. We planned and organized in opposition to the Government, called for strikes and acts of civil disobedience, were harassed and chivvied by the police, banned, and arrested. Then we were locked in prison cells and here I was again, grappling with life in a cell. I did better than that. I spent hours getting behind the political declarations of my characters, dissecting their private inclinations, scrutinizing their love affairs and marriages, their disillusionments and idle talk. When my imagination faltered, I turned again to the Bible. I was ravenous for reading matter. One day during the early part of my stay in Pretoria I was in the yard during exercise hour and saw a scrap of paper in the dustbin for cinders from the kitchen high combustion stoves. I fished it out and held it between my thumb and forefinger to devour the words. It was a prison card and recorded a prisoner's name, number, crime, and sentence. Perhaps a dozen words in all but to me they were like an

45

archaeological find, proof that some people in this society recognized the value of written language. . . .

I played child-like games in my head: going through the letters of the alphabet for names of writers, composers, scientists, countries, cities, animals, fruit, flowers, and vegetables. As the days went on I seemed to grow less, not more, proficient at this game. This was the time I should have been able to feed on the fat of my memory, but I had always had a bad memory (the Security Branch did not believe that one!) and had relied all my life on pencil, notebook, Press clipping, the marking in the margin of a book to recall a source, a fact, a reference. Poetry that I had learned in school fled from me; French verbs were elusive. I lived again through things that had happened to me in the past: conversations and involvements with people, glowing again at a few successes, recoiling with embarrassment at frequent awkwardnesses. I put myself through a concentrated self-scrutiny but in a scattered, disorganized fashion and I found myself not with a clearer insight into myself in this abnormal situation, but with a diffused world of the past diverting me from the poverty of the present. I was appalled at the absence of my inventive and imaginative powers. But I determined to survive by adjusting to a state of enforced hibernation. This was life at quarter-pace. It was a matter of waiting for time to go by, a matter of enduring, an anaesthetizing of self to diminish problems and defeat the dragging passage of days. Life in suspension was the perfect trap for a meandering mind like mine. Day-dreams replaced activity and purposeful thinking. Partly, it was confinement in a vacuum that was doing this to me, but it was partly a succumbing to my own nature and to the difficulty, which I felt acutely, of thinking and composing systematically without the aid of pencil and paper.

The routine activities I could organize for myself were few, and, however I struggled to stretch them out, they were over disappointingly soon and I had to sink back again into inertia. I made the bed carefully several times a day, I folded and refolded my clothes, repacked my suitcase, dusted and polished everything in sight, cleaned the walls with a tissue. I filed my nails painstakingly. I plucked my eyebrows, then the hair from my legs, one hair at a time, with my small set of tweezers. I unpicked seams in the pillow-slip, the towel, the hem of my dressing gown, and then, using my smuggled needle and thread, sewed them up again, only to unpick once more, and sew again. The repetition of these meaningless tasks and the long loneliness made me a prisoner of routines and I found myself becoming obsessional, on the constant look-out for omens. I listened for the sound of motor-car tyres on the gravel road outside the window, tried to guess the make of the car, and then climbed to my observation post to check and to give myself black marks if I were wrong. I found myself arranging bets with myself on the day of the week the Security Branch would call; whether it would be the colonel or the major on inspection duty; whether it would take me ten or fifteen seconds to suck in my breath and then dive under the cold shower in the mornings. I threw pips into a paper bag I used as a waste-paper basket; if I missed Vorster was winning, if I hit the target three times in succession I would be released at the expiry of the first ninety days.

Ninety days. I calculated the date repeatedly, did not trust my calculation, and did it all again. Every day I repeated that little rhyme 'Thirty days hath September' and I counted days from 9 August, the date of my arrest. . . . my calendar was behind the lapel of my dressing-gown. Here, with my needle and thread, I stitched one stroke for each day passed. I sewed seven upright strokes, then a horizontal stitch through them to mark a week. Every now and then I would examine the stitching and decide that the sewing was not neat enough and the strokes should be more deadly accurate in size; I'd pull the thread out and re-make the calendar from the beginning. This gave me a feeling that I was pushing time on, creating days, weeks, and even months. Sometimes I surprised myself and did not sew a stitch at the end of the day. I would wait three days and then give myself a wonderful thrill knocking three days off the ninety.

RUTH FIRST, South Africa, 1963
(from *117 Days*, 1965)

47

Broadening

We were to stay here, who knows how long. Little by little
we lost track of time, of distinctions – months, weeks,
days, hours. It was fine that way. Below, way down,
there were oleanders; higher up, the cypress trees; above
    that, stones.
Flocks of birds went by; their shadows darkened the earth.
That's the way it happened in my day too, the old man
    said. The iron bars
were there in the windows before they were installed, even
    if they weren't visible. Now,
from seeing them so much, I think they're not there – I
    don't see them.
Do you happen to see them? Then they called the guards.
    They opened the door,
pushed in two handcarts full of watermelons. The old man
    spoke again:
Hell, no matter how much your eyes clear up, you don't see
    a thing.
You see the big nothing, as they say: whitewash, sun, wind,
    salt.
You go inside the house: no stool, no bed; you sit on the
    ground.
Small ants amble through your hair, your clothes, into your
    mouth.

YANNIS RITSOS, Greece, 1968
(from *Exile and Return*, 1989)

Rain

This day had been different: the rain had made it different. Shortly after lunch it had begun to rain. The smell of the damp earth made her come to grips with the fact that she was still alive. She inhaled deeply and a rare memory of freedom tickled her cheekbones. The open window let some rain in. A drop fell on her forehead, just above the blindfold, and slowly began to make its way to her heart. Her heart, hard as stone, having shrunk to dodge anguish, finally softened. Like day-old bread soaking in water, her heart was swelling and dissolving. When she thought she was about to cry, she heard her window being closed.

The Little School was full of roof leaks. . . .When almost as many drops had fallen as the days she had spent there they placed cans under the leaks. The first four cans were making the sweetest music she had heard in a very long time. For a while she concentrated on working out the frequency of the drops: *clink . . . clonk . . . plunkplunk . . . clink . . . clonkpluck . . . plunk . . . clink . . . clonk . . . plop.* . . . Can number one was near the back window, the one that had been boarded up. The second can was by Vasca's bed, the third was right in the center of the room, and the fourth was probably by the door frame. Suddenly she heard: *drip . . . drip . . . drip.* . . . She stretched out her hand and the drops found a place in her palm. She treasured five of them in the hollow of her hand, five little pools of freshness and life amid all the dirtiness. She washed her hands. That contact with the water, the first in more than twenty days, made her feel as if she was also washing away some of the bitterness that – mixed with filth – was clinging to her skin. She used the next few drops to wet her lips.

She slept a while, lulled by the sound of the rain, dreaming of tea, fried pastries, and windows framing gray skies that could be seen without a blindfold over her eyes.

ALICIA PARTNOY, Argentina, 1977–1979
(from *The Little School*, 1988)

Breakfast in the Gulag

The air in the mess-hall was as thick as a bath-house. An icy wave blew in through the door and met the steam rising from the skilly. The teams sat at tables or crowded the aisles between, waiting for places to be free. Shouting to each other through the crush, two or three men from each team carried bowls of skilly and porridge on wooden trays and tried to find room for them on the tables. Look at that bloody stiff-backed fool. He doesn't hear. He's jolted a tray. Splash, splash! You've a hand free, swipe him on the back of the neck. That's the way. Don't stand there blocking the aisle, looking for something to filch!

There at a table, before dipping his spoon in, a young man crossed himself. A West Ukrainian, that meant, and a new arrival too.

As for the Russians, they'd forgotten which hand to cross themselves with.

They sat in the cold mess-hall, most of them eating with their hats on, eating slowly, picking out putrid little fish from under the leaves of boiled black cabbage and spitting the bones out on the table. When the bones formed a heap and it was the turn of another team, someone would sweep them off and they'd be trodden into a mush on the floor. But it was considered bad manners to spit the fishbones straight out on the floor.

Two rows of supports ran down the middle of the hall and near one of them sat Fetiukov of the 104th. It was he who was keeping Shukhov's breakfast for him. Fetiukov had the last place in his team, lower than Shukhov's. From the outside everyone in the team looked the same – their numbered black coats were identical – but within the team there were great distinctions. Everyone had his grade. Buinovsky, for instance, was not the sort to sit keeping another zek's bowl for him. And Shukhov wouldn't take on any old job either. There were others lower than him.

Fetiukov caught sight of Shukhov and with a sigh surrendered his place.

'It's all cold. I was just going to eat your helping. Thought you were in the lock-up.'

He didn't hang around: no hope for any left-overs to scrape from Shukhov's skilly.

Shukhov pulled his spoon out of his boot. His little treasure. It had been with him his whole time in the North, he'd cast it with his own hands out of aluminum wire and it was embossed with the words 'Ust-Izhma 1944'.

Then he removed his hat from his clean-shaven head – however cold it might be, he could never bring himself to eat with his hat on – and stirred the cold skilly, taking a quick look to see what kind of helping they'd given him. An average one. They hadn't ladled it from the top of the cauldron, but they hadn't ladled it from the bottom either. Fetiukov was the sort who when he was looking after someone else's bowl took the potatoes from it.

The only good thing about skilly was that it was hot, but Shukhov's portion had grown quite cold. However, he ate it with his usual slow concentration. No need to hurry, not even for a house on fire. Sleep apart, the only time a prisoner lives for himself is ten minutes in the morning at breakfast, five minutes over dinner and five at supper.

The skilly was the same every day. Its composition depended on the kind of vegetable provided that winter. Nothing but salted carrots last year, which meant that from September to June the skilly was plain carrot. This year it was black cabbage. The most nourishing time of the year was June: then all vegetables came to an end and were replaced by groats. The worst time was July, when they shredded nettles into the pot.

The little fish were more bone than flesh; the flesh had been boiled off the bone and had disintegrated, leaving a few remnants on head and tail. Without neglecting a single fish-scale or particle of flesh on the brittle skeleton, Shukhov went on champing his teeth and sucking the bones, spitting the remains on the table. He ate everything – the gills, the tail, the eyes when they were still in their sockets, but not when they'd been boiled out and floated in the bowl separately – great fish-eyes! Not then. The others laughed at him for that.

This morning Shukhov economized. As he hadn't returned to the hut he hadn't drawn his rations, so he ate his breakfast without bread. He'd eat the bread later. Might be even better that way.

After the skilly there was magara porridge. It had grown cold too, and had set into a solid lump. Shukhov broke it up into pieces. It wasn't only that the porridge was cold – it was tasteless when hot, and left you no sense of having filled your belly. Just grass, except that it was yellow, and looked like millet. They'd got the idea of serving it instead of cereals from the Chinese it was said. When boiled, a bowlful of it weighed nearly a pound. Not much of a porridge but that was what it passed for.

Licking his spoon and tucking it back into his boot, Shukhov finished and put on his hat again.

ALEXANDER SOLZHENITSYN, former USSR, 1945–1953
(from *One Day in the Life of Ivan Denisovich*, 1963)

Grass Soup

12 July

In the period when the rule was 'lowered-rations-to-be-substituted-with-gourds-and-greens', vegetables became the main course of the meal, not the side dish. Indeed, people kept themselves going by eating nothing but vegetables. In order not to confuse the reader, I should add that the vegetables we ate were not the kind found on a menu. They were more likely to be found in a textbook on botany. Many varieties were available, like the weeds in the rice paddies; for example, there was just about every kind of grass.

It is true that I enjoy eating all kinds of grass, but I particularly favor bitter green and purslane. Kukucai and dandelions are in the 'composite' family, like chrysanthemums. Dandelion greens have apparently become the rage on the tables of Europe and Japan. At that time we had no inkling of their fashionable future – we knew the plants simply as 'grass', or 'wild green', and we ate a lot of them.

Grass that had been dug from the fields and carted into the kitchen had to go through a process of being picked through before it could go in the pot. The convicts who dug up the plants often handed over roots and all to the kitchen. They knew that they were going to eat these things, but that didn't make them more careful. Like everything else, there was a daily quota on the quantity of greens a convict had to dig up. Leaving the roots and dirt on greens would increase the weight. . . .

'Picking through the green' was not a matter of dividing edible plants from inedible ones. There was no plant that had been dug up and brought in that we wouldn't eat. The term also did not refer to removing dead leaves and crushed stems – if you did that, you were considered unfit for the job and the cook would yell at you. No, 'picking' meant nothing more than shaking the dirt off the plants. And that was a splendid job. It was even better than hauling clods. When I did it, all I had to do was bring along a clod of earth to use as a stool. I would sit beside a great pile of grass, then slowly, slowly, I would shake the plants stalk by stalk. If a piece of bitter greens or purslane was especially juicy and lovely, naturally I would taste it. By the time the greens were picked, I would have eaten my fill.

The weather that day was fine and hot. The sun did its best to shine out over the land and the people on it. I would move my pile of grass and my clod over to a shadier place – I doubt if people sitting under awnings at the beach could have been any more content. A lot of grass would already be limp and shrivelled after being dug up, carted to the kitchen and left for a while. What I ate, however, was generally buried in the middle – it was grass that still exuded the moist fragrance of the earth. What's more, after being sealed in the middle of the pile, the juicier plants would sometimes have begun a natural fermentation.

In the outside world, people used to joke about a poor man who pretended to be living in luxury. Every time he finished eating, he would wipe his mouth with pork rind, so that when he went out people would think he'd just eaten meat. Here in the camps, the trick would be to see whether or not a convict's mouth was green. He would be envied and considered a lucky man if he had any chlorophyll on his lips.

ZHANG XIANLIANG, China, 1960
(from *Grass Soup*, 1994)

Forcefeeding

On Wednesday afternoon, the fifth day without food, the sister came to my cell with a gaunt, elderly man dressed in a safari suit – an attractive matching combination of light-weight shirt and shorts or trousers which white men and some Africans wear in Rhodesia. They are known, by Africans, as the Rhodesian Front uniform.

The man introduced himself as Dr Baker Jones. I hope and believe that during most of that period I managed to keep a tight rein on all my internal fears, and that they did not show on my face. But when I heard his name I relapsed into the same kind of inward panic I had felt when I was being taken from Marandellas to a destination unknown.

In November 1970, an inquest was held on a detainee and prominent African leader, Leopold Takawira, who had died in prison. It was found that his death was due to undiagnosed diabetes. The doctor responsible for him was Dr Baker Jones. . . .

He examined me and took my blood pressure. Throughout this time we kept up a desultory conversation. He became more and more friendly. When he tapped my knees for reflexes he said, 'You're as bad as I am.'

'Is that very bad?' I asked.

'Oh, I'm just an old alcoholic,' he replied. Each time I saw him his breath was heavy with whisky. I felt sorry for him and wondered how the Takawira case had affected him.

On Thursday afternoon he came back with the sister, a buxom hard-mouthed lady. They went through the ritual of weighing me and testing my blood pressure and then Dr Baker Jones announced that I was in critical condition and that he could not let me die.

I was very surprised. This was the sixth day without food and I felt in good health, far better than I had during the first few days. . . .

Dr Baker Jones sat on the bed again.

'Will you eat?'

'No.'

'Then we have no alternative but to force feed you.'

There was a long silence.

'Will you resist?'

I tried once more to explain why I was on a hunger-strike and said that I wasn't trying to inconvenience the people who had me in their care.

'Do you really think Mr Lardner-Burke even knows you're in prison?' asked the sister.

'I know he does,' I replied. 'He signed my detention order.'

She snorted. 'I can tell you,' she said, 'that Mr Lardner-Burke is as much responsible for you being here as the Minister of Health is for the rats in Harare Hospital.'

Dr Baker Jones seemed encouraged by this line of conversation. He stood up and looked at me with a new unfriendliness. . . .

The cell filled with people, including a medical orderly aptly named Mr Large. He looked the most human of the lot. . . . They put a blanket over me and asked once more if I would resist. I said I would not as my battle was with the Smith regime, not them personally, and I was sorry that they were involved at all. Then in a last appeal, I asked them if they had heard of the Nuremburg trials where it was ruled that it was not always an adequate defence simply to do one's duty. . . .

Mr Large applied a gag to keep my mouth open. Then the sister started screwing a long tube down my throat. I suppose I simultaneously started crying. The tube hurt badly and no one had explained that it had to be forced right down into the depths of my body. I understand it all now, of course, and know that the tube has to be forced down past a muscle which closes off the stomach. But then I had no idea what they were doing. I was choking, crying, pouring with sweat and, I was quite sure, drowning. I simply could not breathe.

'Breathe through your nose! Breathe through your nose!' the sister kept ordering, although she must have realized my nose was blocked.

The doctor stood behind the sister with a ewer and started pouring a thick white mixture down the tube through a funnel. The funnel blocked. I was quite sure that by now I was indeed, as Dr Baker Jones had asserted, in a critical condition. The cell, blazing with electricity, was turning black.

I pulled my hands out from beneath the blanket and, as what they got into me came up, I yanked the tube out of my stomach. I was prepared to be forcefed. I was not prepared to be asphyxiated. I lay in the mixture, choking, coughing, gasping for breath. The same procedure was repeated so many times that, losing consciousness, I lost count.

Eventually Dr Baker Jones said that he knew I was not vomiting deliberately and that they were going to inject me, to relax my muscles. There was a general lighting up of cigarettes and some of them left the cell while the sister injected me. The doctor's hands were shaking.

In what seemed to be a very short time they all trooped back and tried again, and again. One of the most humiliating parts of the exercise was a mental struggle I was fighting: as I was attempting to cooperate, Mr Large had little to do. One of his hands lay empty and relaxed on the bed beside me and it was all I could do not to hold it.

At some point, Mr Large said that it was 4.45 p.m. and that he was supposed to have been off duty at four. They packed up their equipment and prepared to leave, saying they would be back the next day. It flickered across my mind that Dr Baker Jones had been lying. If I was in a critical condition they would not be leaving me with nothing inside me.

Dr Baker Jones's estimation of my present condition was such that before *he* left he ordered the prison personnel to ensure that nothing was left in my cell with which I could commit suicide.

Then the medical party went away.

JUDITH TODD, former Rhodesia, 1972
(from *The Right to Say No*, 1972)

Peanuts and Sesame Cakes

The first day, all we had was a little water, nothing else. By evening I began to feel hungry. But I tightened my belt buckle and lay down very early, just staring at the ceiling. After a while I got tired and fell asleep.

The second day, I woke up very early, probably because of my hunger pangs. Fortunately, I had my emergency rations next to my pillow. I reached in, grabbed some peanuts and counted out twenty. I put one in my mouth, which had a wonderful taste, and held it there as long as I could. I spent five or six minutes on each one. Ah, those beautiful peanuts! They were the elixir of life, they were lifesaving pills. Having eaten all twenty, I took stock – my store was visibly reduced. If I ate twenty each time, six more meals and my 137 peanuts would be gone! I regretted my action and was angry at myself for not listening to 'nutritionist' Zhang Yunqing's advice to wait until the third day.

A hungry man pays particular notice to his neighbor's mouth, observing him with unusual acuteness and sensitivity. I discovered that Old Zhang, lying motionless on his wooden bed, also seemed to have something in his mouth. So now I had found a way to rationalize my error, and I felt better. No matter what, though, those twenty peanuts I'd eaten were gone forever.

The third day of the strike began. According to Old Zhang, this was the crucial day, and it was all right to eat a little more. I was terribly hungry, and in the morning I ate half a sesame cake. To my dismay, the cake seemed to increase my appetite, and I couldn't help departing from my original plan. I began to nibble at the edges of the second half, like a silkworm working away at the edges of his precious mulberry leaf. Gradually the cake stopped resembling a half-moon and took on the shape of a thinner and thinner crescent. When there was only a thin crescent left, I began to get upset, for I was eating two days' worth of food in one sitting. What would I do later on? That afternoon I ate twenty more peanuts and drank a lot of water. By nightfall I was still hungry. I told my cellmates how I was feeling, and

Xiao Wenguang criticized me. 'Remember, from now on no one is allowed to talk about how hungry he is, or to say that something tastes good.' There was nothing I could say.

The even more sophisticated 'nutritionist' Zhang Yunqing admonished us. 'Remember, no one should talk unnecessarily. Moving your lips and tongue consumes calories. . . . What I just said probably burned over a peanut's worth of calories.' Everyone laughed, but Old Zhang remained very serious, not even cracking a smile. Perhaps laughing consumed calories too.

That afternoon the medical officer came and went through the motions of checking blood pressure, listening to hearts, and feeling foreheads. 'You're destroying your own bodies,' he said in a sympathetic voice. 'What's the point? Tell me your demands and I'll go speak to the warden. If you keep striking you'll get sick, and I'll be too busy to help anyone.'

Teacher Xu told him, 'Please report to the new warden that we have four demands: we won't eat bad rice; we want better vegetables and oil in the vegetables; we want a piece of meat each week; and we want permission to read magazines and journals.'

The medical officer nodded. 'I'll tell him.'

Old Zhang sat up from his bed. His forehead was beaded with sweat. 'No more beatings and abusing the prisoners. The shackles put on during the strike must be taken off!'

'All right, I'll tell him.'

That night I was too hungry to sleep. I had eaten quite a bit that day so why was I still so hungry? There was nothing to be done – I reached into my bag and pulled out a peanut. It tasted wonderful, but I couldn't stop taking another and another. . . .

That afternoon, the fourth day, was the worst. I can still remember the taste. My mouth kept secreting saliva, very bitter saliva. But when I went to spit it out I found my mouth was dry. The bitter taste was coming from the coating on my tongue. I also felt the emptiness in my stomach begin to spread to my spine. . . . What does it feel like? If you haven't been through this kind of hunger yourself, it's almost impossible to comprehend. Basically, it feels like your whole body is about to disintegrate any minute; it feels like your legs are floating, suspended in mid-air. . . . The strange thing was that my brain wasn't affected at all by the hunger. It kept working away, and in fact seemed to be working harder than ever. My head remained clear throughout and I was acutely aware of every sound and every disturbance outside. Unfortunately, this meant that the hunger too was particularly sharp, and this made it impossible to escape the pain.

The fifth day approached slowly, terribly slowly. But finally it arrived . . . I observed the movements of the others and noticed that Old Zhang still had some peanuts left. When he finished off the last one he heaved a weak and regretful sigh. His forehead oozed large beads of sweat. Xiao Wenguang's beriberi began to act on his legs. The way he staved off hunger was to hold some water in his mouth to try to make himself feel as if he were eating something. I noticed that Teacher Xu was eating his last slice of ricecake. His face was as ashen as a piece of white paper and his eyes were shut tight. If not for the faint movement of his mouth you might have thought he was dead. Taking in this frightful scene, I grew quite disheartened. Guo Shouqi was also lying there as still as a corpse, letting the sunlight from the window shine on him. He looked like a statue of a sage. . . .

At four o'clock that afternoon, two head guards brought a notice from the warden which they read loudly several times: 'In response to prisoners' requests, we are going to improve the quality of the food; supply better quality rice; add one piece of meat each week.'

'Wasn't there one more demand?'

'What demand?'

'Allowing us to read magazines and journals.'

'That one isn't on the list,' he said. 'I'm afraid the municipal party office won't agree. But the warden has already spoken with the educational officials. We will allow your relatives to bring any journals you want, so long as they're legal publications.'

Teacher Wu's face took on a little color. He smiled. I tearfully embraced him, shouting happily, 'We won! We won!'

WANG RUOWANG, China, 1934–1937
(from *The Hunger Trilogy*, 1991)

You Left Me My Lips

You took away all the oceans and all the room.
You gave me my shoe-size with bars around it.
Where did it get you? Nowhere.
You left me my lips, and they shape words, even in silence.

OSIP MANDELSTAM, former USSR, 1935
(anonymous translation)

Castles and Banquets

When sent to the 'box' (punishment cell), I would try to smuggle in a fragment of pencil lead, usually by hiding it in my cheek. Then I could spend my time drawing castles – on scraps of newspaper or directly on the floor and walls. I set myself the task of constructing a castle in every detail: from the foundations, floors, walls, staircases and secret passages right up to the pointed roofs and turrets. I carefully cut each individual stone, covered the floor with parquet or stone flags, filled the apartments with furniture, decorated the walls with tapestries and paintings, lit candles in the chandeliers and smoking torches in the endless corridors. I decked the tables and invited guests, listened to music with them, drank wine from goblets, and lit up a pipe to accompany my coffee. We climbed the stairs together, walked from chamber to chamber, gazed at the lake from the open veranda, went down to the stables to examine the horses, walked round the garden – which also had to be laid out and planted. We returned to the library by way of the outside staircase, and there I kindled a fire in the open hearth before settling back in a comfortable armchair. I browsed through old books with worn leather bindings and heavy brass clasps. I knew what was inside those books. I could even read them.

This was enough to occupy me for my entire spell in the 'box', and still there were plenty of problems left over to solve the next time; it was not unknown for me to spend several days trying to decide on the answer to a single question, such as what picture to hang in the drawing room, what cabinets to put in the library, what table to have in the dining room. Even now, with my eyes closed, I can retrace that castle, in every detail. Some day I shall find it – or build it.

Yes, some day I shall invite my friends and we shall cross the drawbridge over the moat, enter these chambers and sit at the table. Candles will be burning and music playing, and the sun will gradually set behind the lake. I lived for hundreds of years in that castle and shaped every stone with my own hands. I built it between interrogations in Lefortovo, in the camp lock-up and in the Vladimir punishment cells. It saved me from apathy, from indifference to living. It saved my life. Because one must not let oneself be paralysed; one cannot afford to be apathetic – that is precisely when they put you to the test. It's only in sport that referees and competitors wait for you to reach your best form – records achieved that way are not worth a damn. In real life they make a point of testing you – to the limit – when you are sick, when you are tired, when you are most in need of a respite. At that point they take you and try to break you like a stick across their knees! And that's the very moment, whilst you are still groggy, when the godfather, the KGB security officer, hauls you out of your cellar, or the political instructor invites you in for a chat.

Oh no, they won't put it to you point blank, suggesting that you collaborate. They need much less than that for now – just some trivial concessions. They simply want to accustom you to making concessions, to the idea of compromise. They carefully feel you out, to see if you're ripe for it. Not yet? Okay, go back to your cellar, there's still plenty of time to ripen, they've got decades ahead of them.

Idiots! They didn't know that I was returning to my friends, to our interrupted conversation before the fire. How were they to know that I was talking to them from my castle battlements, looking down on them, preoccupied more with how to fix the stables than with answering their stupid questions? Laughingly I returned to my guests, firmly closing the massive oak doors behind me.

It is at moments when you lapse into apathy, when your mind grows numb and can think of nothing better to do than gloomily count the days till your release – it is precisely then that someone in the next cell is taken ill, loses consciousness and collapses on the floor. You ought to hammer on the door and demand that a doctor be sent. In return for that hammering and commotion the enraged prison governor will undoubtedly prolong your stay in the punishment cell. So keep your mouth shut, shove your head between your knees, tell yourself you were asleep and heard nothing. What business is it of yours? You don't know the man, he doesn't know you, you will never meet. And you might very well not have heard.

But can a castle-dweller permit such behaviour? I lay my book aside, pick up a candlestick and go to the gate to admit a traveller who has been overtaken by bad weather. What does it matter who he is? Even if he's an outlaw, he must warm himself at my hearth and spend the night under my roof. Let the storm rage outside the castle – it can never tear off the roof, penetrate the thick walls or extinguish my fire. What can it do, the storm? Only howl and sob down my chimney.

VLADIMIR BUKOVSKY, former USSR, 1971–1976
(from *To Build a Castle: My Life As a Dissenter*, 1978)

Doodling

Fantasy

I have no control over my circumstances, but I can describe and interpret them. There is at least this measure of mastery I have over my fate. Thoughts flit and tumble elusively. Over the days and weeks I develop certain ideas. They have no solidity: fragments of dreams and fantasies drift, eddy and disappear through my brain. One day it is a whole theme that presents itself, the next a vision of people, the third merely a word that repeats itself over and over like a radio advertisement. The scaffolding of my thought is weak, but gradually it assumes a meaningful form. . . .

I will write a book. What happens to me will be mere chapters in the story. This is a way of fighting back. The worse things they do to me, the more interesting the book will be.

Yet a book is too flat, too controlled, too wordy and abstract. It requires pencil and paper and calm surroundings. In a book the material of life is rolled flat and sliced up into two-dimensional pages. I want something better, more immediate. . . .

I will write a play. A stage has volume, people standing up, people talking and a live crowded audience. I get up off my mat, put on trousers and a shirt and walk to and fro in the cell, thrilled as I develop the project.

On the stage will be three apparently opaque cubes. As the play develops, each cube will light up to reveal its inhabitant. I visualize the cubes. Perhaps they will be on different levels, so as to emphasize our present spacial disorientation. My cell could go anywhere, at any time, a space-capsule above the earth, or a submarine resting below the icecap. . . .

The vision of the three cubes fades and my thoughts tumble away from the stage. I try vainly to direct them back to the play I will write. I wish it were easier to concentrate. . . .

Pen and paper

The paper is dazzlingly white and in my hand is a pencil. The wood feels clumsy between my fingers. I must use it, but to do what? I rest my hand on the pad and wait for my fingers to start moving. Should I write my name? But that would be silly. Should I draw something? But I am hopeless at drawing. The pencil point is on the paper now at the top right hand corner of the page. Slowly it presses up and down on that spot. The lead markings are like a small pit of charcoal. My first creation is taking place. There it is: a tiny black blob. Is that blob me, all hunched up, secretive and anonymous? Is it my cell, so small, sealed and impregnable? This blob is an adventure, a probing. . . .

I do not want to waste paper so I start off in the corner. Yet I have plenty of paper and can always get more. The law has now guaranteed me my supply. I have hidden a bit of broken off pencil and they will never find it in this fluff-covered cranny in the corner of my window frame. I will keep it there, just in case.

Ah, that is a bit better. I have now drawn a square, small but with an empty space of white in the middle. I suppress an urge to black it in. I must draw more freely, more happily, for am I not blessed to have pencil and paper? Yet my fingers are unpractised and stiff, as though the nerves which lead from them to the brain are stiff with dirt and decay. In addition there is an unseen rein holding my hand in check, stopping it from crossing the page in the bold, sweeping movements that would more accurately represent the conscious excitement of my mind. I am unused to the freedom of writing. I have the opportunity to write, but am helpless to utilize it. I am early man learning to write, a child making its first marks. . . .

Never mind, I tell myself, in time you will uncoil and after a few days you should be able to make better use of these writing materials.

Activities

My writing progress has been slow. I am not short of time, of course, and in terms of the court order I am entitled to receive a reasonable supply of writing materials. Yet I have produced very little. It has taken me over two months to start on something other than word games.

For the first few days all I could do with pencil and paper was to jot down requests to the station commander. Then I started thinking out word games and only now have begun anything that approaches creative writing. I will not get far with my writing. Apart from my inherent inadequacies, I am held back both by lack of incentive and by fear that what I write will be seized.

It is difficult to write without directing my thoughts to someone who will read the script. Yet now I must write for no one. It is writing in the air, mere exercise not unlike my physical jerks. I do it because I know it is good for me. It helps keep my mind in trim. Thus . . . everything I put down on the paper is neutral. Abstract drawings, word games, crossword puzzles – I have a folder full of pieces of that kind. There are no deep thoughts, no descriptions of my new world, no commentaries on life as a prisoner. I have thought out nothing new, nor reformulated anything old. My special thoughts, the insights I have gained, the new emotional depths I have sounded within myself, all these must remain secret until I come out. The police must never be allowed to see into my mind. They must never be allowed to get hold of and to crush my thoughts, for the police are book-burners, destroyers of things delicate. There is only one safe place for my thoughts: in myself. . . .

When I look at the folder of scrap paper, I see I have collected pages of word ladders. From jail to free in the fewest number of steps, changing one letter at a time, there are seven links in the chain: Jail – fail – fall – fell – feel – feet – fret – free.

ALBIE SACHS, South Africa, 1963–1964
(from *The Jail Diary of Albie Sachs*, 1964)

I Have Stopped in Front of Time

Suddenly
I have stopped in front of time:
the days come down in vain stalactites
because it's not exactly a tunnel
but it's an emptiness of existence
where everything useless goes rolling to the depths.
It's like that here. . .and it's more than like that.
And it can't be understood except with our flesh
thrust into this hollow
which is cruelty, as certain
as flour of anguish for the only food.
Hatred had a face only in this enclosure.
This isn't in the statistics
or in the hymns.

I am only the outline of a poem
between iron bars and shadow,
a voice that they've tried to strangle
with mutes. . . .

Your body, shunning contact,
is the space into which fall
the letters of your name,
and time is shattered.

ANGEL CUADRA, Cuba, 1967–1982
(translated by Donald Walsh)

Writing on Toilet Paper

To hell with the warders! Away with intruding thoughts! Tonight I don't want to think about warders and prisoners, colonial or neo-colonial affairs. I am totally engrossed in Wariinga, the fictional heroine of the novel I have been writing on toilet paper for the last ten months or so!

Toilet paper: when in the sixties I first read in Kwame Nkrumah's autobiography, *Ghana*, how he used to hoard toilet paper in his cell at James Fort Prison to write on, I thought it was romantic and a little unreal, despite the photographic evidence reproduced in the book. Writing on toilet paper?

Now I know: paper, any paper, is about the most precious article for a political prisoner, more so for one like me, who was in political detention because of his writing. For the urge to write is almost irresistible. At Kamiti prison, virtually all the detainees are writers or composers. . . . Now the same good old toilet paper – which had been useful to Kwame Nkrumah in James Fort Prison and to Dennis Brutus on Robben Island, and to countless others with similar urges – has enabled me to defy daily the intended detention of my mind. . . .

A week after my incarceration, Wasonga Sijeyo, who had been in that block for nine years but had managed to keep a razor-sharp mind and a heart of steel, eluded the vigilant eyes of the warders then guarding me and within seconds he told me words I came to treasure:

It may sound a strange thing to say to you, but in a sense I am glad they brought you here. The other day, in fact a week or so before you came, we were saying that it would be a good thing for Kenya if more intellectuals were imprisoned. First it would wake most of them from their illusions. And some of them might outlive jail to tell the world. The thing is, just watch your mind. Don't let them break you and you'll be alright even if they keep you for life. But you must try. You have to, for us, for the ones you left behind.

Thus in addition to being an insurrection of a detained intellect, writing this novel has been one way of keeping my mind and heart together like Sijeyo.

Free thoughts on toilet paper! I had resolved to use a language, Kikuyu, which did not have a modern novel: a challenge to myself and a way of affirming my faith in the possibilities of the languages of all the different Kenyan nationalities. . . . Easier said than done: where was I to get the inspiration? A writer needs people around him. He needs live struggles of active life. Contrary to popular mythology, a novel is not a product of the imaginative feats of a single individual but the work of many hands and tongues. A writer just takes down notes dictated to him by life among the people, which he then arranges in this or that form. For me, in writing a novel, I love to hear the voices of the people working on the land, forging metal in a factory, telling anecdotes in crowded matatues and buses, gyrating their hips in a crowded bar before a jukebox or a live band, people playing games of love and hate and fear and glory in their struggle to live. I need to look at different people's faces, their gestures, their gait, their clothes, and to hear the variegated modulations of their voices in different moods. I need the vibrant voices of beautiful women: their touch, their sighs, their tears, their laughter. I like the presence of children prancing about, fighting, laughing, crying. I need life to write about life.

But it is also true that nobody writes under circumstances chosen by him and on material invented by him. He can only seize the time to select from material handed to him by whomever and whatever is around him. So my case now: I had not chosen prison, I was forced into it, but now that I was here, I would try and turn the double-walled enclosure into a special school where, like Shakespeare's Richard II, I would study how I might compare:

This prison where I live unto the world. . . .

In the daytime, I would take hasty notes on empty spaces in any book I might be reading, I would scribble notes on the bare walls of my cell, then in the evening I would try to put it all together on toilet paper.

Sometimes I would be seized with the usual literary boredom and despair – those painful moments when a writer begins to doubt the value of what he is scribbling or the possibility of ever completing the task in hand – those moments when a writer restrains himself with difficulty from setting the whole thing on fire, or tearing it all into pieces, or abandoning the whole project to dust and cobwebs. These moments are worse in prison because there are no distractions to massage the tired imagination: a glass of beer, a sound of music, or a long walk in the sun and wind or in a starry night. But at those very moments, I would remind myself that the ruling class had sent the novel to me so that my brain would turn into a mess of tot. The defiance of this bestial purpose always charged me with a new energy and determination: I would cheat them out of that last laugh by letting my imagination run loose. . . .

Later

Kenyatta's death, another dream of freedom possessed us all. . . . A rumour started: we would be freed on Friday, 22 September. The morning of Friday, 22 September, found us still in the grips of hope. There had been no official word, but the rumour had become a reality. Why not? Every reasonable argument pointed to our release on that day. Some detainees had sat down, made a list of all cabinet members and tried to determine their voting pattern in terms of *yes* and *no* to our release on that day and naturally, the ministers in favour of our release outnumbered those against us. A detainee who cautioned realism in our expectations was shouted down and denounced.

It was a kind of collective madness, I remember, and when at about ten o'clock there was a vigorous banging on the outer door and a prison officer dashed in waving his staff of office, I said to myself, At long last: God, freedom.

Quickly, Koigi pulled me aside and whispered: 'Go and clean your room at once! There is going to be a search!'

No sooner were the words out of his mouth than we were all hounded back to our cells: if this meant release, then it was certainly a rough way of bidding us farewell.

I had never seen a prison search before and though the other detainees told me that under Lokopoyot it had been a weekly ritual, I never really knew what it meant. My cell was the first to be raided: it was difficult to know what they were looking for. Razor-blades, nails, weapons of violence? Letters, diaries, secret communications with the outside world? Suddenly the sergeant saw piles of toilet paper and pounced on them. Then, as if delirious with joy and triumph, he turned to the presiding officer and announced: 'Here is the book, sir, on toilet paper.' 'Seize it!' the officer told him, 'The whole lot! Who told you to write books in prison?' the officer said, turning to me.

My novel written with blood, sweat, and toil on toilet paper had been seized! Only two chapters hidden in between the empty back pages of a bible Koigi had lent me remained. The bible lay there on the desk as if mocking me: 'If you had trusted all the Wariinga novel to me, you would have saved it all.'

It is only a writer who can possibly understand the pain of losing a manuscript, any manuscript. With this novel, I had struggled with language, with images, with prison, with bitter memories, with moments of despair, with all the mentally and emotionally adverse circumstances in which one is forced to operate while in custody – and now it had all gone.

Gloom fell over Kamiti. Every detainee had lost something. We had been deliberately lulled into slumber by the carefully circulated rumour of release. But most detainees had developed a fantastic cunning which had made them act like lightning and many had saved a lot of their prison notes. I had suffered the major loss and the other detainees clearly felt for me. I was grateful for the group solidarity. But it didn't lessen the hurt.

The next three weeks were the worst of my stay at Kamiti. It was as if I had been drained of all blood. Nevertheless, I made a new resolution: no matter what happened I would start all over again. I would reconstruct the novel in between the printed lines of a Chekhov. . . . It would not be the same novel, but I would not accept defeat.

I never had occasion to try out my resolution, though I did scribble the plot and the few sequences of events I could recollect in Chekhov's volume of short stories – *The Lady with a Lap Dog* – for, after about three weeks, on 18 October, the new S.S.P. returned the Wariinga manuscript to me.

'I see nothing wrong with it,' he said. 'You write in very difficult Kikuyu!' he added.

'Thank you,' was all I said. But he will probably never know the depth of emotion behind those two words. Nor perhaps what his action meant for the birth of a new literature in Kenya's languages.

NGUGI WA THIONG'O, Kenya, 1978
(from *Detained*, 1981)

Man on the Moon

One after another, winters without heat replaced stifling bug-infested summers. Time melted into nothingness, marked only by the reactions of my body to mere temperature. I was becoming both more spiritualized and bestial. Never were storms so violent, so desired, so remembered; they raged inside me, leaving in their wake a serene calm.

Fancifully debauched and exhausting bouts of sleeplessness alternated with forbidding, indelible dreams. Every morning the penitentiary bell would shake me out of bed, worn-out and shattered, my mind in a jumble. It took all my forces to jerk myself back to reality – to the monotony of prison life. Later, after the morning walk, I was driven by a need to sit down behind a small rickety pine table and write. Even if I did not feel like it at times, I could not put it off. Not only would a failure to write deprive my imprisonment of any meaning, it would also weigh heavily on me as a kind of betrayal of myself and my idea.

Undoubtedly, the Party leaders, whom I had known as friends and coworkers for many years, wished to put me out of action even as a writer. The administration being content to forbid me writing paper, however, I wrote on toilet paper, a humiliation that only intensified my neurotic, passionate 'obligation' to write.

A prison is an appropriate and fruitful place for reflection – especially for abstract, utopian, 'cosmic' reflection.

In the fall of 1957 – on the very day that the first human artifact broke loose from Earth's gravity as a Soviet capsule soared into extraterrestrial space – policemen came to the penitentiary at Sremska Mitrovica to take me away. I was to be tried because of a book I had written. The reward for being yanked out of prison for this trial was a sentence of seven additional years in prison. I had already completed almost the whole first year of my previous sentence, a punishment for my solidarity with the Hungarian uprising of 1956.

I was writing a novel, *Montenegro*, at the time, precisely that passage where the hero, Milos, is waiting to be hanged with two fellow victims. The contemplation of all these extra years of imprisonment spawned the blackest of thoughts and, indeed, sensations of a morbid horror. At the

72

same time, news of man's breaking free from this earthly 'vale of tears' could not help but evoke thoughts of man's cosmic destiny. Along the road over which they transported me to the city, life bubbled – little boys with hoops, women still in summer dresses and light sweaters, workers in rumpled, grimy clothing. The frayed, yellowed leaves of already ripened corn were enveloped in haze and dew. And a bull was on the scene, huge and powerful, tethered by an iron ring through its nostrils being led to market or to the slaughterhouse by a peasant straight out of the Middle Ages.

After the trial, they brought me back to Sremska Mitrovica by another road. I was completely drained and sorrowful, but calm and ready for new insights, new ideas. . . .

Man – is he or is he not a cosmic being? . . . By penetrating into the Cosmos, Man, or his instruments, have already begun an epoch of scarcely dreamed possibilities. With its escape from Earth's fetters, mankind embarks upon its immortality.

The most majestic and most terrible drama in the history of Man is underway. In going forth into infinity, Man has consigned himself to an endless prison as well as to boundless freedom. Even as prison will appear ever more endless, the freedom will beckon ever more unattainably. Penetration into the spatial prison will augment inner freedom, however.

The future of Mankind lies in the far reaches of the Cosmos, but tragedies of unimagined, monstrous proportions and forms await him there. Mankind will spread out but eventually manage to unite on cosmic battlefields. Today's ideas, today's dogmas and pragmatic ideologies will crumble away in terrestrial dust. The cosmic future belongs to ideas, philosophies, and religions. Man's happiness will seem more attainable than ever, for his possibilities will appear limitless. Before us lies an epoch of leaders and thinkers, dreamers and realists, of such elan and depth of vision as mankind has never seen.

Thoughts such as these possessed me in prison. Because of its narrow confines, prison encourages one's thoughts to roam to overcome circumstances and natural laws, and to abandon themselves to their own limitless freedom. In a prison no barriers are imposed between the cell and infinity, between the idea and reality. . . .

Since one is freest in prison, being released from prison is no simple matter.

MILOVAN DJILAS, former Yugoslavia, *c.* 1956
(from *Of Prisons and Ideas*, 1986)

The Blind Architect

I decided to write a book about my wife's eyes. It would be entitled *Risha's Eyes in the Cell without a Number*. Curiously, I wasn't thinking about my wife as such, for that would have been acutely painful, but was organizing myself, like a poet at his work table, before undertaking some inspired professional endeavor. I held a long discussion with myself about what style to employ. Modeling it after Pablo Neruda would be reiterative, an inadequate romanticism, perhaps; whereupon I recalled Federico Garcia Lorca's style in 'Poet in New York', and came up with a few lines, but then began wondering if perhaps Stefan George's symbolism might not be more appropriate, for in a certain way it was linked with Franz Kafka's world. But if my quest were to end here, that meant that my mental writing had to begin. And the important thing was for that task to last as long as possible. I recalled the work of Chaim Nachman Bialik, particularly one of his poems about a pogrom, but his work struck me as being too peculiar to eastern European experience; as for Vladimir Maykovsky, he seemed overly Russian in his love poems to Lila Brick and too verbose in his poetry about the Russian Revolution. I likewise dismissed Paul Éluard; Claudel was unadaptable, and Aragon didn't especially impress me. There remained, of course, the poets of my youth: Walt Whitman, Carl Sandburg, and the Spaniards Miguel Hernández and Luis Cernuda. Finally, I settled on Stephen Spender, and began to write, in my mind.

One might think that the selection of style would bring back memories of the times when I first read those writers. Memory is the chief enemy of the solitary, tortured man – nothing is more dangerous at such moments. But I managed to develop certain passivity-inducing devices for withstanding torture and anti-memory devices for those long hours in the solitary cell. I refused to remember anything that bore on life experience – I was a professional stoic dedicated to his task. The book I was working on absorbed me for days, though now I can't remember a single line. For a time I recalled paragraphs, but now they are profoundly buried. And the thought that they may resurface is as frightening as the notion of reliving those solitary hours.

Some day I suppose I'll be forced to re-encounter myself by way of all that. Perhaps I'm experiencing the same problem as Argentina, an unwillingness to be aware of one's own drama.

Another activity of mine was to organize a bookstore. I thought about how one day I'd be free, figuring that several long years might elapse before that moment, maybe ten or fifteen. Thinking in terms of a prolonged span of time is extremely useful when there is no fixed sentence, for it annihilates hope, and hope is synonymous with anxiety and anguish. I imagined my eventual arrival in Israel and the need to organize some work. I decided that a bookstore would be the most suitable way for two voracious readers like myself and my wife to earn a living. I speculated on all the details: the size of the main room, the name, the typography of the letters printed on the windows, the type of books we'd sell, whether it would be a good idea to install a literary salon on an upper floor or perhaps an experimental film society. A detailed task of this sort could easily keep me occupied for days. Following the same method, I organized a newspaper in Madrid, another in New York, my life on a kibbutz, and a film by Ingmar Bergman on the solitude of a tortured man.

Long afterwards, I realized that I had developed a withdrawal technique. I tried through every available means, while inside my solitary cell, during interrogations, long torture sessions, when only time remained, all of time, I tried to maintain some professional activity, disconnected from the events around me or that I imagined to be going on around me. Deliberately, I evaded conjecture on my own destiny, that of my family, and the nation. I devoted myself simply to being consciously a solitary man entrusted with a specific task.

The peephole of my cell opens and the face of the corporal on guard appears. He smiles, and tosses something into the cell. 'Congratulations, Jacobo,' he says.

I am startled. . . . The sound that just dropped into my cell has destroyed the puzzle and doesn't fit into the despair of the cell, nor into my effort to compensate for that despair by my slow, laborious, ardent reconstruction of the exterior architecture, the blind man's stubborn obsession with his puzzle.

I pick up a letter and two candies. The letter, a few brief lines, is from my wife. Dated 20 May 1977. We've been married today for twenty-seven years. I leave everything on the bed and go back to my task as blind architect: She's undoubtedly contacted one of our army friends, one of those who came to our house so often, or one of the retired officers who worked on my newspaper, perhaps someone who spent vacations at our beach house; and yet, this doesn't fit into the heightened sensibility of a blind man whose sightless eyes are gazing at an unknown world. No military man nowadays would dare to speak to my wife. More likely one of the policemen, a ward guard, went to visit her and offered, for a sum of money, to bring something to me. At this point the blind architect starts reconstructing the scene. My house, the entrance, the doorbell, my wife's face – but no, the image of my wife's face is unbearable in this place.

How I cursed my wife that day! How many times I told myself I wouldn't read her letter, I wouldn't eat the candies. After so many efforts to forget, to refrain from loving and desiring, to refrain from thinking, the entire painstaking edifice constructed by the blind architect collapses over his head. Already, I'd begun to belong to the world around me, the one I actually belonged to, the imprisoned world where my heart and blood were installed: this world I've already accepted and that is real, that corresponds to the inscriptions on the wall, the odor of the latrine matching that emitted by my skin and clothes, and those drab colors, the sounds of metal and violence, the harsh shrill, hysterical voices. And now this world, so heavily armored, so solid and irreplaceable, without cracks, has been penetrated by a letter and two candies. Risha, why have you done this to me?

She tells me that if she could she'd give me heaven with all its stars and clouds, all the air in the world, all her love, all her tenderness. She says that she'd kiss me a thousand times if she could. But that is what she fails to understand: she cannot. In a rage, I throw the letter into the latrine, and with equal rage stick the two candies into my mouth. But already I'm lost, for the flavor is overpowering, as is my wife's face.

JACOBO TIMERMAN, Argentina, 1977
(from *Prisoner without a Name, Cell without a Number*, 1981)

A Form of Protest

In the political camp, the prisoner starves for an outlet to his feelings even more than in the criminal camp. On one occasion or another he gets a spell in the cooler and on the way there gets beaten up in the guardroom by the warders. He starts to write official complaints, but is soon convinced that this is useless. Meanwhile, he has a long term ahead of him; and he has brought his own forms of protest with him from the underworld, together with its customs and points of view. This is where the tattoos come in.

Once I saw two former criminal cons, then politicals, who were nicknamed Mussa and Mazai. On their foreheads and cheeks they had tattoos: 'Communists = butchers' and 'Communists drink the blood of the people'. Later I met many more cons with such sayings tattooed on their faces. The most common of all, tattooed in big letters across the forehead was: 'Khrushchev's slave' or 'Slave of the CPSU' (Communist Party of the Soviet Union).

In the special regime camp, in our hut, was a fellow called Nikolai Shcherbakov. When I first caught sight of him in the exercise yard through the window I almost collapsed; there wasn't a single clear spot on his whole face. On one cheek he had 'Lenin was a butcher' and on the other it continued, 'Millions are suffering because of him.' Under his eyes was 'Khrushchev, Brezhnev, Voroshilov are butchers.' On his pale, skinny neck a hand had been tattooed in black ink. It was gripping his throat and on the back were the letters CPSU, while the middle finger, ending on his Adam's apple, was labelled KGB.

Shcherbakov was in another corner cell similar to ours, only at the other end of the hut. At first I only saw him through the window when their cell was taken out for exercise. Later, though, we were transferred to another cell and we often exercised simultaneously in adjoining yards. In secret conversations, unnoticed by the warders, we got to know one another. I became convinced that he was normal and not cracked, as I had thought at first. He was far from stupid: he used to read quite a lot and knew all the news in the papers.

In late September 1961, when our cell was taken out for exercise,

Nikolai asked us in sign language whether anyone had a razor blade. In such cases it is not done to ask what for – if somebody asks, it means they need it, and if you've got one, you hand it over, no questions asked. I had three blades at the time hidden in the peak of my cap; in spite of all the searches they had never been found. I went into the latrines, ripped open the seam under the peak with my teeth and took out one blade. Back in the yard, when the warder's attention was distracted, I stuck it into a crack on one of the wooden fence posts to which the barbed wire was secured. Nikolai watched me from his window. The blade stayed there in the crack all day long. Many other cons saw it – the boys used to scour every corner of the exercise yard while outside, every pebble, every crack, in the hope of finding something useful. But once a blade has been placed somewhere, that means it already has an owner waiting to pick it up; in such a case nobody will touch it. Furthermore Nikolai spent the whole day at the window, keeping watch on the blade just in case. While exercising the following day, he picked out the blade and took it back to his cell.

Later that evening a rumour passed from cell to cell: 'Shcherbakov has cut off his ear.' And later we learned the details. He had already tattooed his ear: 'A gift to the 22nd Congress of the CPSU.' (Evidently he had done it beforehand, otherwise all the blood would have run out while it was being tattooed.) Then, having amputated it, he started knocking on the door, and when the warder had unlocked the outer door, Shcherbakov threw his ear through the bars to him and said: 'Here's a present for the 22nd Congress.'

This incident is now well known to all cons in Mordovia.

The next day we saw Shcherbakov at the window of his cell. His head was bandaged and in the place where his right ear should have been the bandage was soaked with blood, and blood was on his face, neck, and hands. A couple of days later he was taken to hospital, but what happened to him after that I do not know.

Shcherbakov's cellmates were all hauled in for helping him – for taking part in anti-Soviet propaganda.

And that is why cons always have to be without their caps during inspection and to uncover their foreheads, so that they can be checked for tattoos. Men with tattoos are first sent to the cooler and then put in separate cells, so as not to corrupt others. Wherever they go after that they are always accompanied by a special section in their files, listing the location and texts of their tattoos; and during inspections the tattoos are checked against these lists to see whether any new ones have been added.

How do cons in the cooler and in prison contrive to tattoo themselves? How do they get the needles and ink? I have often seen it done, both in special regime camps, in transit camps and in Vladimir prison. They take a nail out of their boots or pick up a scrap of wire in the exercise yard, sharpen it on a stone – and there's your needle. Then to make the ink, they set fire to a piece of black rubber sole from their boots and mix the ash with urine.

But it wasn't the technique that astonished me so much as the very idea of the activity. What did these unfortunates want? Why and to what end did they deform themselves for life? For to do that was to brand yourself for ever, to brand your whole life, it meant you felt yourself to be, in the words of the song, 'an eternal convict', if you disfigured your face . . . or cut off an ear. Why?

But sometimes, in moments of helpless despair, I too caught myself thinking: my God, if only I could do something – hurl a piece of my body into the faces of my torturers!

Why? At such moments, the question doesn't arise.

ANATOLY MARCHENKO, former USSR, 1961
(from *My Testimony*, 1969)

Wild Geese, Tell My Mother

Since not too long ago, in the town of Seoul
A strange sound repeating itself incessantly has been heard,
A strange weird sound.
There are some people who, each time
    they hear the sound, shake
Like an aspen leaf and shed cold sweat.

. . .

Kung . . .
That's it. . . . Kung
What's that sound?

. . .

So they brutally shoved the fellow An-Do
into a solitary cell.
Click
The locks were locked, and while the locking sound
echoed farther and farther he continued to cry,

'No, no, no, no. What has been done to me?
I was clad in rags, and starved, worked,
Beaten and oppressed, but did not utter
    a word of protest.
I didn't rest, didn't lie down, didn't even sleep,
And yet what have they done to me ?
What devilish crime did I commit to bring upon
    me a punishment so severe?
You wild geese flying up in the sky,
    do you know how I feel?
Can you tell me whether my mother is standing
    on the new road near our shack
Waiting for my return?

Is she weeping soundlessly, looking in the
    direction of Seoul, wearing her out-of-season
    clothes?
Wild geese, tell my mother
I will return,
I will return even if I am dead –
Even if my body is torn into one thousand
    or ten thousand pieces.
I will break out through the walls of this jail,
    I'll leap over the fence
Even if I have to sell my soul to the devil.
I will return, mother, whatever happens, I will return.'

And then An-Do wanted to sing, but he had no
    head. He wanted to cry, but he had no eyes.
He wanted to shout, but he
    had no voice.
With neither voice nor tears,
    he cried soundlessly
    day after day, night after night,

. . .

An-Do rolled over and over,
Back and forth from wall to wall,
    Kung, back
and forth from wall to wall, continuously,
Kung
and one more time Kung and again
Kung
Kung
Kung

KIM CHI HA, South Korea, 1972–1974
(from 'Groundless Rumors' in *Cry of the People*, 1974)

The True Prison

It is not the leaking roof
Nor the singing mosquitoes
In the damp, wretched cell
It is not the clank of the key
As the warden locks you in
It is not the measly rations
Unfit for beast or man
Nor yet the emptiness of day
Dipping into the blankness of night
It is not
It is not
It is not

It is the lies that have been drummed
Into your ears for a generation
It is the security agent running amok
Executing callous calamitous orders
In exchange for a wretched meal a day
The magistrate writing into her book
A punishment she knows is undeserved
The moral decrepitude
The mental ineptitude
The meat of dictators
Cowardice masking as obedience
Lurking in our denigrated souls
It is fear damping trousers
That we dare not wash
It is this
It is this
It is this
Dear friend, turns our free world
Into a dreary prison

KEN SARO-WIWA, Nigeria, 1993

A Child's Drawings

They didn't have any lists when they took us out for work assignments – just stood us in groups of five, since not all the guards knew their multiplication table. Any arithmetical computation is tricky when it has to be done with live objects in the cold. The cup of convict patience can suddenly overflow, and the administration knew it.

Today, we had easy work, the kind they normally reserve for criminals – cutting firewood on a circular saw. The saw spun, knocking lightly as we dumped an enormous log onto the stand and slowly shoved it towards the blade. The saw shrieked and growled furiously. Like us, it detested working in the north, but we kept pushing the log forward until it split into two, unexpectedly light pieces.

Our third companion was chopping wood, using a heavy blue splitting axe with a long yellow handle. He worked on the thicker pieces from the ends, chopped the smaller ones in half with one blow. He was just as hungry as we were and the axe struck the wood in a feeble fashion, but the frozen larch split easily. Nature in the north is not impersonal or indifferent; it is in conspiracy with those who sent us here.

We finished the work, stacked the wood, and waited for the guards. Our guard was keeping warm in the building for which we'd been chopping wood, but we were supposed to march back in formation, breaking up in town into smaller groups.

We didn't go to warm up, though, since we had long since noticed, next to a fence, a large heap of garbage – something we could not afford to ignore. Both my companions were soon removing one frozen layer after another with the adroitness that comes from practice. Their booty consisted of lumps of frozen bread, an icy piece of hamburger, and a torn pair of men's socks. The socks were the most valuable item, of course, and I regretted I hadn't found them first. 'Civvies' – socks, scarfs, gloves, shirts, pants – were prized by people who for decades had nothing to wear but convict garb. The socks could be darned and exchanged for tobacco or bread.

I couldn't reconcile myself with my companions' success, and I too began to use my hands and legs to break off brightly colored pieces of the garbage pile. Beneath a twisted rag that looked like human intestines, I saw – for the first time in many years – a blue school notebook.

It was an ordinary child's drawing book.

Its pages were all carefully and diligently colored, and I began turning the bright cold naive pages, grown brittle in the frost. I also used to draw once upon a time, sitting next to the kerosene lamp on the dinner table. A dead hero of fairy tale would come alive at the touch of the magic brush, as if it contained the water of life.

Looking like women's buttons, the water colors had lain in their white tin box, as Prince Ivan galloped through the pine forest on a gray wolf. The pines were smaller than the wolf and Prince Ivan rode him like an Eskimo on a reindeer, his heels almost touching the moss. Smoke spiralled into the blue sky, and the neat Vs of birds could be seen among the stars.

The more I strained to recall my childhood, the more clearly I realized that it would not repeat itself and I would not encounter even a shade of it in the drawing book of another child.

This drawing book was a frightening one.

The northern city was wooden, its fences and walls painted in a bright ocher, and the brush of the young artist faithfully duplicated the yellow color wherever he wanted to show buildings and creations of man.

In the notebook there were many, very many fences. The people and the houses in almost every drawing were surrounded by even, yellow fences or circumscribed with the lines of barbed wire. Iron threads of the official type topped all the fences in the child's notebook.

Near the fences stood people. The people in the notebook were not peasants or hunters; they were soldiers, guards and sentries with rifles. Like mushrooms after the rain, the sentry booths stood at the feet of enormous guard towers. On the towers soldiers walked, their rifle barrels gleaming.

It was a small notebook, but the boy had managed to paint into it all the seasons of his native town.

The ground was bright and uniformly green, as in paintings by the young Matisse, and the blue, blue sky was fresh, pure, and clear. Sunrises and sunsets were conscientiously crimson, and this was not childish inability to capture half-tones, color shifts, or shading. Nor was it a Gauguin-type prescription for the art where everything that gave an impression of green was painted in the best green color.

The color combinations in the schoolbook were a realistic depiction of the sky in the far north where colors are unusually pure and clear and do not possess half-tones.

I remember the old northern legend of how God created the taiga while he was still a child. There were few colors, but they were childishly fresh and vivid, and their subjects were simple.

Later, when God grew up and became an adult, he learned to cut out complicated patterns from his pages and created many bright birds. God grew bored with his former child's world and he threw snow on his forest creation and went south for ever. Thus went the legend.

The child remained faithful in his winter drawings as well. The trees were black and naked. They were the enormous deciduous trees of the Daurian Mountains, and not the firs and pines of my childhood.

The northern hunt was on, and a toothy German shepherd strained at a leash held by Prince Ivan. . . . Prince Ivan wore a military hat that covered his ears, a white sheepskin coat, felt boots and deep mittens. Prince Ivan had a submachine gun over his shoulder. Naked, triangular trees were poked into the snow.

The child saw nothing, remembered nothing but the yellow houses, barbed wire, guard towers, German shepherds, guards with submachine guns, and a blue, blue sky.

My companion glanced at the notebook and rubbed a sheet between his fingers.

'Find some newspaper if you want to smoke,' he said. He tore the notebook from my hands, crumpled it, and threw it onto the garbage pile. Frost began to form on it.

VARLAM SHALAMOV, former USSR, 1937–1954
(from *Kolyma Tales*, 1982)

Time Stands Still

Anyone who didn't discipline himself, who didn't concentrate his attention on some steady object of study, was in danger of losing his reason, or at least of losing control of himself. When subjected to such total isolation and absence of daylight, given the monotony and the constant cold and constant hunger of prison life, a man tended to fall into a kind of half-conscious trance. For hours and maybe even days on end he would sit there, gazing with unseeing eyes at a photograph of his wife and children, or leafing through the pages of a book, taking in and remembering nothing, or else he would suddenly start an endless, senseless altercation with one of his neighbours over some totally trivial issue, bogging down repeatedly in the same arguments, not bothering to listen to what his opponent was saying and in fact not answering his objections at all. He would find it absolutely impossible to concentrate on anything definite or follow the thread of an argument.

Strange things happened to time. On the one hand it seemed to pass with preternatural speed, beggaring belief. The entire daily routine with its ordinary, monotonously repetitive events – reveille, breakfast, exercise, dinner, supper, lights out, reveille, breakfast – fused into a sort of yellowish-brown blur, leaving behind nothing memorable, nothing for the mind to cling to. And lying down at night, a man would be at a loss to remember what he had been doing all day, what he had eaten for breakfast and what for dinner. Worse still, the days would become indistinguishable from one another and be completely erased from your memory, so that when you woke one day, as if someone had jogged you, you would realize: Christ, it's bath day again! That meant that seven or sometimes even ten days had flown by. And so you lived with the sensation that you were getting a bath everyday. On the other hand, this same time could crawl with agonizing slowness: it would seem as if a whole year must have gone by, but no, it was still the same old month, and no end was in sight.

Then again, a man could go into paroxysms of rage if something interrupted his monotonous routine. One day, for example, at the start of a new month, they would suddenly take you out for exercise, not after breakfast but after dinner instead. What difference, you might ask, would such a little thing make? But this was enough to drive men into frenzies. Or you had a row with one of the guards, or were called out by the instructor and lost your temper with him – and now you couldn't read and couldn't sleep and couldn't think of anything else. The book swam before your eyes, you couldn't keep your mind on anything and you would be trembling all over. So what, you might say. Nothing new about any of this. How many of these arguments and quarrels, how many rows with the guards had you had in your time? Too many to count. Still, for days and nights afterwards you would continue to relive it all in your mind – what he said, what you said, what you might have said but didn't because you couldn't think quickly enough. And how you might have found a particular way of getting under his skin or stopping him dead in his tracks or finding answers that were more cutting and convincing. Like a scratched gramophone record this dialogue would go round and round in your head, and there was no way of stopping it. Or else you would get a picture postcard from home and sit there staring at it like an idiot, the bright colours so exotic and enticing that you couldn't tear your eyes away.

VLADIMIR BUKOVSKY, former USSR, 1971–1976
(from *To Build a Castle: My Life as a Dissenter*, 1978)

The Day Your Letter Comes

The days are so fierce
there's no difference between them
and there have been so many years
of these identical days
so that the day your letter comes
is an almanac event

that day a name is born to time
so much so that the days
have ended up being classified
into nameless days
and the day your letter comes

your letter is the poem brought by the dawn.

it seemed as though today was the day
there were heralds and signals
a sunless shine climbed up the walls
there was wounded music in the barbed wire
and it must have been then
that they broke your letter's wings

like a carrier pigeon which the falcons intercepted

inside the envelope
the word smothered
like an abortion
beauty created
for nobody

night falls like a curtain
everything goes back to being like it was
in front of my cell

nameless
endless
days
go by

ANGEL CUADRA, Cuba, *c.* 1979
(translated by Donald Walsh)

A Letter from My Father

We've got no letter from you for so long –
we badly want some news of you.
In brief I'll tell you how things are at home.
Mother's gone purblind in both eyes,
so night and day she hangs around the house.
I'm not much more than an old dotard now,
my legs all doddering as I step.
Just to address an envelope, I must think hard!
I wish you were at home to help us out.
Thinking of you, we always weep,
not knowing if you're still at the old camp,
or if you've been moved to somewhere else.
Mother keeps asking in her prayers
that you stay safe and sound, not sick.
When you receive this letter, see to it
that you write home – we want to hear from you.
Alas, that in your young and foolish days
you thought wrong thoughts, argued and complained!
You must in all sincerity now repent:
only then will the Party pardon you
and we can hope to see you once again
before we both pass on.
We just don't know what more to say –
let us remind you: nurse your health.
You're still so young!
You'll surely live, my son.
We yet believe that heaven and earth
won't play havoc on good, simple folks.
The other day I went to the post office
and mailed you my own pair of socks.
As for the medicine you asked me for,
I'll have to wait till my next pension pay.
I'll buy and send it then in case you're sick.

In closing, I do hope you will compete
and be the first at laboring for your camp.
                            Your father and mother

NGUYEN CHI THIEN, Vietnam, 1967
(from *Flowers from Hell*, 1984)

Stefica

I had been married to Stefica not quite four-and-a-half years – of which almost three had been spent under the stress of surveillance – when Tito decided in November 1956 to get rid of me by sending me off to prison.

Neither at the time of my arrest, nor throughout nine succeeding years of imprisonment – with a break of little over a year on probation – did I once doubt Stefica's devotion and steadfastness. If even the shadow of a suspicion came my way momentarily, I knew its source to be that darkness of prison loneliness which magnifies human depression and depravity. This trust was more the result of Stefica's being the kind of person who arouses no doubts rather than because of my own nature, even though I am not a doubter. Moreover, even our three-year-old son Aleksa, who was exposed to the horrors of retaliation as a result of my imprisonment, was at that time no more than a fateful blood-tie linking me to Stefica's devotion.

To be sure, Stefica was also bound to me through the idea. So many others, incomparably more prominent than she, had severed all ties as if I were a curse. In Stefica's devotion, however, ideas, no matter how loyal she was to them, served only as a complement to our marriage. Stefica's devotion would have failed only if I had done something truly immoral, something trespassing acceptable limits of human weakness. Very secure in her own ideas, she was also capable of adjusting her moral stance, of accommodating herself to new conceptions as a part of her own being as well as of our relationship.

During the time we endured my imprisonment together, my memory of her person was never separated from my image of her, all her characteristic qualities. Her grey-blue eyes admonished me with a reproachful sadness in my moments of despair; her wonderfully lovely hands offered me comfort; her open smile, her dimples and gleaming teeth banished my sorrows and cares.

Because of Stefica, with her and through her, the tie between my prison cell and the outside world was not broken. The world continued to live in me and I in it. And it was through this contact that I became more real to myself, and my imprisonment was able to assume a more lasting, even higher meaning. This was not so much because Stefica visited me regularly with Aleksa and catered to my unspoken whims and needs, as because of her dauntless, courageous, steadfast personality. I saw her as myself in the outside world. As more than myself, in fact. I saw her as that part of myself that would endure, that would hold fast to the mainstay of life and the essence of the idea.

I knew that as long as I had Stefica, nobody, nobody, could endanger me. It was doubtless her presence and the knowledge of her vigil that helped dispel the fear that I might be 'swallowed up in darkness' or covered by a 'veil of oblivion'. Whenever I think of death – and prison is a terrible breeding ground of dark reflections – the thought would come to me that with Stefica I would outlast even death. I believed, I knew that Stefica would be with me both in death and after death.

In time, a prisoner gets used to prison, especially if his is a long sentence, so that every departure from the monotony disturbs and flusters him. That is what I came to experience, in time, from Stefica and Aleksa's visits. No matter how much I yearned to see them and prepared myself inwardly for our meetings, I would return to my cell after these reunions devastated. The suppressed and stifled part of my life would erupt, convulse and bleed. In my passionate attachment to both, I was not able to think of them as being separate. The two together cared for me and watched over me. It was this bond that fretted and cried out, yearning for its fulfillment, its revivification.

MILOVAN DJILAS, former Yugoslavia, 1956
(from *Of Prisons and Ideas*, 1986)

The Correspondence between Halil and Aysha

On the second floor of the prison, Halil
   sat looking out the window at the night
     and wrote a letter to Aysha, his wife:

'My love . . .
I can feel your hair
singing in my hand.
You're six hundred kilometers away, and here
   so near . . .
But that's a whole other subject.
In this year 1941
   we won't talk about us two,
I'm not that brave yet . . .

My love,
look how the electric light
   outside the white
     house by the road burns blue
       through the masking paper.
The road is bright under the moon.

In the induction center yard, the armory
   and the trees –
     acacias, plums, and mulberries.
There's also an arbor,
   which I can't see.

It's the first of August.
The nights are still short.
The guardsmen whistle.
The road is deserted.
Clouds drift through half the sky.

That's the Zonguldak train
   roaring by.
Despite the moon,
in the other half of the sky
   I can see stars
     above the mountains.
The train just crossed the iron bridge
   behind the poplars.
  . . .

The new town is near the station.
Its blue lights glow through the trees.
I hear a woman's voice,
children shouting. There's a lump in my throat:
   I miss my daughter so.

The shadows of two men
   walking side by side
     slowly
        passed by.
They were officials, I think,
   very somber and tired.
They mustn't have been talking. . . .

The train pulled out,
its whistle piercing
   like ears ringing.
I hope your ears are ringing, my wife. . . .'

Writing his wife, Aysha,
by the window
on the second floor of the prison, Halil
   left his letter in the middle
and read – maybe for the fifth time –
   the letter he'd received from her that morning.
And he felt free and happy, like flowing water.
Aysha wrote in her letter:
'I'm lying on the cushion by the window,
with a blanket over my knees.

I'm quite cozy.
I can see fields –
   wonderful fields –
      and Chamlija Hill.
The air is so still.
Sounds make terrific echoes.
They're plowing a field right next to our garden:
two oxen,
a man in front pulling,
and another in back holding the plow.
The earth swells up,
big with life under the human hand.
I watch, amazed.
What an enormous,
   difficult task!
How can they do it so easily,
   so simply?
They've resurrected a huge patch of earth since morning.
Let's see what they'll plant.
I'll write and tell you.
Night's coming on:
"The crows are flying home from school."
We used to say that when I was a child.
Your daughter, Leyla, says it, too.
It's gotten dark.
I lit the lamp
and looked in the mirror.
A woman whose husband's in prison is always looking
   in the mirror,
always.
More than any other woman
   she's afraid of getting old.
She wants the man she loves to like her when he comes out,
no matter
   if it's thirty years later.
The woman in the mirror isn't old yet:
her hair is red,
   and her eyes
      are now green,
         now honey-colored.'

Halil folded Aysha's letter
and put it in his pocket.
And he continued the letter he'd left in the middle:
'My only one,
of course your hair is red,
and yes, your eyes
  are now green,
  now honey-colored!
Anyone could have seen it.
But I was the first
  to see their colors,
    because I was the first to put them in words.
And that
is all I've written that wasn't said before
  in the world. . . .
Yes, your hair is red,
and your eyes
  are now green,
    now honey-colored.
And there's something else you may not be aware of:
your hands are wonderful.

. . .

My only one,
I thought we wouldn't talk about us two
  in this year 1941.
There's the world,
  our country,
    hunger, death,
      longing,
        hope and victory,
and now, along with and part of
  our country and the world,
  there's the two of us with our separation and our love.'

NAZIM HIKMET, Turkey, 1941
(from *Human Landscapes*, 1982)

97

Halfway Mark

Dear Olga,

Today I have served half my sentence....

When I was still in Hermanice, something happened to me that superficially was in no way remarkable, but was nevertheless very profoundly important to me internally: I had an afternoon shift, it was wonderful summer weather, I was sitting on a pile of iron, resting, thinking over my own affairs and at the same time, gazing at the crown of a single tree some distance beyond the fence. The sky was a dark blue, cloudless, the air was hot and still, the leaves of the tree shimmered and trembled slightly.

And slowly but surely, I found myself in a very strange and wonderful state of mind: I imagined I was lying somewhere in the grass beneath a tree, doing nothing, expecting nothing, worrying about nothing, simply letting the intoxication of a hot summer day possess me. Suddenly, it seemed to me that all the beautiful summer days I had ever experienced and would yet experience were present in that moment; I had direct, physical memories of the summers I spent in Zdarec as a child; I could smell the hay, the pond, and I don't know what else (as I write this, it seems like a parody of a passage from one of my plays – but what can I do? And anyway, isn't parody often merely an attempt at self-control by stepping back a little from oneself and one's secret emotions?).

I seemed to be experiencing, in my mind, a moment of supreme bliss, of infinite joy (all the other important joys, such as the presence of those I love, seemed latent in that moment), and though I felt physically intoxicated by it, there was far more to it than that: it was a moment of supreme self-awareness, a supremely elevating state of the soul, a total and totally harmonic merging of existence with itself and with the entire world.

So far there was nothing especially unusual about this. The important thing was that because this experience, which contrasted so entirely with my prison-house/ironworks reality, was more sudden and urgent than usual, I realized more clearly something I had felt only dimly in such moments before, which is that this state of supreme bliss inevitably contains the hint of a vaguely constricting anxiety, the faint echo of an infinite yearning, the strange undertone of a deep and inconsolable sense of futility. One is exhilarated, one has everything imaginable, one neither needs nor wants anything any longer – and yet simultaneously it seems as though one had nothing, that one's happiness were no more than a tragic mirage, with no purpose and leading nowhere. In short, the more wonderful the moment, the more clearly the telltale question arises: and then what? What more? What else? What next?. . . It is, I would say, an experience of the limits of the finite; you have approached the outermost limits of the meaning that your finite, worldly existence can offer you and for this very reason, you are suddenly given a glimpse into the abyss of the infinite, of uncertainty, of mystery. There is simply nowhere else to go – except into emptiness, into the abyss itself. . . .

I think everyone must have experienced this at some time: in a moment of supreme happiness, it suddenly occurs to you that there is nothing left now but death (a feeling, by the way, that has entered into common speech, for we say, 'I love you to death,' 'See Naples and die,' etc.).

This vague anxiety, this breath of infinite nonfulfillment emanating from an experience of the greatest fulfillment, this sensation of terrifying incomprehensibility that blooms in a moment of firmest comprehension, can always be brushed aside like a bothersome piece of fluff. You may wait till the cloud temporarily covering the sun passes by and go on living in peace and delight without asking troublesome questions. But you may also do the opposite: forget about all the 'spontaneous meaningfulness' that gave you such intense pleasure, forget about the answer given before the question was posed and stop precisely at the point where the cold air from the abyss struck you most powerfully – when you felt most intensely that in fact you have nothing, know nothing, and, worst of all, do not even know what you want – and bravely confront the question that comes to mind in such moments. That is, the genuine, profound and essentially metaphysical question of the meaning of life.

There it is: I'm trying to write about the meaning of life and so far I've done no more than make repeated efforts to define the questions more precisely, or rather the existential circumstances in which it takes hold of one.

Well, there's no hurry. I still have quite enough prison Saturdays and Sundays ahead of me. At least as many before me as behind me.

VACLAV HAVEL, former Czechoslovakia, 1979–1983
(from *Letters to Olga*, 1987)

Letter to the Boys

Dear boys,

You must now be in Kazimierz, roaming through gorges and walking along the banks of the river Vistula. Please say hello to all the familiar haunts, to all the homes we've visited together and to all my friends. Perhaps you will already be back in Warsaw by the time you get this letter. I've no way of knowing. Perhaps we may even see each other before this letter reaches you.

For the past two weeks the whole prison has been buzzing with talk of amnesty and the possibility that most of us will be set free. But since we will be let out by the same people who locked us up, it is difficult to foresee their criteria and order of priority for release. So don't waste your time waiting for me outside the prison gates! Especially as they've already done the dirty on us: younger children than yourselves have already been granted visits to see their dads, and we haven't even been allowed to see each other through two thick screens. So I'm not wasting time waiting for anything: I'm getting on with my doctorate, reading and taking notes.

I'm leading a very rich social life. After spending three days in a cell for two I landed up in another for five days, together with Joasia's father. Since July 15 I've been among totally new company again. Every move produces new, interesting people, new experiences, and new ways of spending twenty-four hours closed up within the wall of 'clink', as they dub prison here.

There's a Jewish saying: 'May you live in interesting times!' (That is, times during which, as you may suspect, there's a greater likelihood of getting knocked on the head!) The prison equivalent would be, 'May you live in interesting times, and have no better company than that you are forced to keep.' Luckily, those who are thrown into the 'clink' are not generally boring: whether it be a worker from the Ursus tractor factory, or a historian who went to the same school as me, we always manage to find common ground for discussion.

I exercise daily, lifting buckets of water, doing knee bends (no running for lack of space!). I can't allow myself to go flaccid like the pierced balloon which burst on Piglet as he ran along with it to Eeyore's birthday party, can I? Nor can I be like overstretched underpants elastic the next time we go boating on the lakes, setting up camp on successive islands. Do you remember that awful rain that caught us unawares on the Wigry lakes, just as we were drying ourselves in the meadow by the bridge? And that atoll in the middle where we could dive straight from the boat because the water was so shallow? And your last swimming feats with Mum on that windy day by the footbridge on the Wigry lakes?

I remember everything. And don't worry: all these good times will return. Life is short, but not so short as not to allow us to ramble around Poland together again. Meantime, I send you all my love. Be good to each other and help Mummy. Have some ice cream for me – and go and see a nice film.

Your Daddy

CzesŁaw Bielecki, Poland, 1983

Letters to Josephine

Dear Jo –

Snow tonight, the first of the winter. It was mostly mixed with rain earlier but managed to get itself straightened out by the time we were coming back to our dormitory from supper at around half-past five – The mop-handle felt kind of good in my hands this morning – Monday, Wednesday and Friday are mop days – and I realized I'd been looking forward to it: I guess either I was feeling good or I'm going crazy – or both – The radio rumor about our appeal turned out to be true: the Circuit Court upheld our convictions last Tuesday with one small dissenting voice occupying itself with some sort of technicality which may (or may not) do us an eansy-weansy bit of good in a strictly academic way. We've got a couple of days to decide whether we'll go up to the Supreme Court with it, I dare say there'll be lawyers down to see us next week, but I won't be too broken-hearted if mine can't make it – We drew our winter underwear this afternoon, but I'm not likely to feel ambitious enough to bathe and get into them tonight – The pictures of Ann walking around in the pale coveralls were wonderful as most of her pictures are – I don't have to tell you, I hope, how glad I am your doctor can't find much wrong with you beyond the usual ravages of age and how I am looking forward to your second offspring. You're a nice girl, that's what you are, and I love you – The local talent has just left for the auditorium where they'll rehearse for an amateur show to be given presently. Most of the inmates here are from the hills of this state, West Virginian and Tennessee – guitars and hillbilly music are likely in for one hell of a beating – Give my love to everybody and especially to you and Lily and Ann.

Some days later

Dear Princess –

I let last week slide by without writing you. I don't know whether laziness was to blame or short-term slackness or a combination. It's easier and easier to tell myself there's no use writing when I'll soon be talking to you on the phone – only you're not to start thinking the same thing. Your letters have been wonderful and you're a darling and you're by all means to keep them coming to the last minute – L. is not coming to meet me and my airplane transportation from Charleston, W. Va. (which is only a couple of hours from here by bus), is either to be mailed me here ahead of time or be waiting for me at the airport in Charleston. Will you check this with L. for me? Anyway, I should be in NYC plenty of time for Sunday night's dinner and I'll phone you at such time as I imagine you come home from your roaming but are not yet in the hay – The Supreme Court was to have heard our tale of woe last week and we may get some sort of peep out of them this week or next. They aren't going to do me, personally, a hell of a lot of good at this late date, but I'm a fellow who's mighty grateful – so I say – for any small crumb that falls my way – The news from L. was very good in that it all sounded very Lillianesque and she doesn't always sound Lillianesque unless she's in good spirits – I still haven't – and won't have until I've had a chance to look the situation over in NYC – any idea of what I'm going to do when I get out or when I'm coming to California. Being in jail is really being out of the world, since even your friends seem to think they're helping you by not telling you anything that might 'worry' you, and, even when they do try to tell you something, they are either so cryptic, or so take for granted your knowledge of things you don't know, that you can't make heads or tails of what they're saying – Much love to you, honey, and give my love to all especially not forgetting L and A –

Pop

DASHIELL HAMMETT, USA, 1951

Marwa, My Daughter

When I had left home, my infant daughter Marwa was still six months old. I disappeared from her sight and mind in a way I will never forget. She remains my special secret. It was she who taught me, from the moment of her birth, not to prefer boys to girls.

On that last morning, I remember, I woke from an anxious dream. I got out of bed silently and crept to her crib. I pulled the blanket back to reveal her warm, red face and her smile, her sleepy smile. I was surprised when she opened her eyes and surprised again when her smile widened. She looked as if she had been longing for me. I drew closer to her, I stared at her. She was like an oasis to a parched traveller. How could I ever abandon her? Her tiny fingers worked their way from under the blanket and up to my face.

Ah, my daughter, the four months from that last morning until your first visit to me in Ramleh Prison were full of the flash of that last smile. Each time my imagination caused the cell walls to crumble, each time my mind made its way up the open road, the first thing I saw ahead of me were the features of your tiny face in every detail. How I feared they would change before I next saw them – doesn't childhood fall away so rapidly?

Now, today, you sat on the other side of the meshed screen and glanced at me with total indifference. The indifference cut me to the quick. I recalled your former features with lightning speed and was astonished at the changes. You were here for only thirty minutes, but I relive them now as if chapter and verse of a holy scripture. . . .

You sat looking at me. As if I hadn't been the one to play with your hair. As if I didn't desire the touch of your fingers. As if I hadn't bathed you in warm water nor told you stories before you knew what stories were. And as if I was not angered by how my absence had erased my picture from your mind.

O Marwa . . . my appeals were pointless, the ice of your indifference would not melt. I did not see anger in your face, only the hesitation which comes from fear. Who is this man who stands behind the fence, who is this man who is begging me to remember moments he believed were not just fleeting? You avoided my kiss, ignored my call and remained indifferent, even to the shouts of the policeman who declared the visit over.

On my way back to my cell, no one addressed me save to say, 'How was the visit? Nice?' It was enough to make me contemplate sealing off my world. . . . In my mind, I found myself standing at the entrance to the refugee camp to which I was brought as a child. This, then, was the world, this was reality, normality, sanity: it was as if the tin shacks were, after all, of our own making. As if the sewage and stench were of our own choosing. As if we were hungry because we fasted voluntarily. As if illness were a matter of happenstance. And as if God had stopped trying and had closed the doors of mercy.

IZZAT GHAZZAWI, Israel and the Occupied Territories, 1990 (from *Point of Departure: Letters from Prison*, 1993)

Ruth v. the Torturer

For a while now I've been trying to recall how Ruth's face looks. I can remember her big eyes, her almost non-existent little nose, the shape of her mouth. I recall the texture of her hair, the warmth of her skin. When I try to put it all together, something goes wrong. I just can't remember my daughter's face. It has been two months since I've seen her. I want to believe she's safe.

'Vasca! Do you remember my daughter's face?' I whisper.

'Of course I do, she's so pretty.'

I think I'll turn over in my bed. That will help me reorder my thoughts. No, it doesn't work. It's funny. I can recall the things we did together, even when I'm not thinking about them all the time; but I want to imagine her face, to put together the pieces of this puzzle.

The other day, after the big rain, the guard brought a puppy into our room. He allowed me to keep it on my bed for awhile. It was playful and sweet, like my baby. . . .

Perhaps if I try to bring to mind some scenes when we were together; for example, that day while coming back from my parents: I was pushing her stroller along the street when suddenly she looked up at the roof of a house. An immense dog was impatiently stalking back and forth. Ruth pointed to the dog with her little finger. 'Meow,' she said, since she was used only to watching cats climb up high. Thrilled, I kissed her – but how did her face look? I can only remember her small, triumphant smile.

Night is coming. The radio is on, not very loud this time, playing Roberto Carlos' song again. When the newscast starts, they turn the radio off.

One morning, while on the bus, I heard on the radio:

Fellow citizens, if you notice family groups traveling at odd hours of the day or night, report them to the military authorities. The number is. . . .

I was one of a few passengers on that early bus. It was 6.30 a.m. I was traveling to a suburban neighborhood with my baby and two bags. For a short while I thought the driver was going to stop the vehicle and run to the nearest phone to alert the army. He just glared at my reflection in the rear view mirror. The night before some friends of mine had been kidnapped. Since they knew where I lived, I thought of moving out for a few days, just to be safe. But I can't remember my daughter's face on that bus. I know that she was wearing the pink jacket, and that I had the bag with stripes, the one my Mum used to take to the beach. I have a perfect recollection of everything in the bag. But try as I might, I still can't remember my daughter's face. I could describe her toys, her clothes. If only I had her picture. But again, maybe it's better this way. If I could look at a picture of her face, I would surely cry. And if I cry, I crumble.

Later

Daughter, dear, my tongue hurts and I can't say *rib-bit, rib-bit*; even if I could, you wouldn't hear me. This little poem soothed you when you cried; you went to sleep listening to it. . . I've repeated it for a whole day, but I still can't sleep. *Rib-bit, rib-bit, he sings on the roof* . . . I won't see you again. . . . Trapped, like the little frog . . . *but we hear him all the time*. I told the torturers if they took me to the meeting place I would point to him. Then, when I saw him, I didn't do what I'd promised. Afterward, the electric prod again and the blows . . . harder: 'Where is he?' But my child. . . . *Rib-bit, rib-bit*. . . . Where are you, my little girl? 'I don't know where he is.' The punch to my stomach. Stop it . . . please! Like a caged animal. *We hear him all the time / Rib-bit, rib-bit, little frog* . . . if only I was a frog. I smell like a caged animal. I think I'm about to lose my mind. *Nobody knows where he hides*. . . . If I fall asleep I won't ache for a while . . . I guess a whole day has passed . . . I'm going to recite the poem to you again, my girl, the poem of the little frog. . . . Soon you'll be two years old and you'll learn it all. *We all hear him when it rains/Rib-bit, rib-bit*. . . . *Nobody's seen him at home*. . . . My girl, my tongue is hurting and I can't say *rib-bit, rib-bit* . . . but this poem soothed you when you cried . . . don't make me believe I'm an animal . . . that's not my scream . . . that's some animal screaming . . . leave my body in peace. I'm a little frog for my daughter to play with . . . she'll soon be two years old and she'll learn the whole poem. . . . *We all hear him, rib-bit, rib-bit, when it rains, rib-bit, rib-bit*. . . .

ALICIA PARTNOY, Argentina, *c.* 1975
(from *The Little School*, 1988)

Where I Am There Is No Light

Where I am there is no light
and it is barred.
Just beyond
there lies a lighted space.
Therefore light must exist.
Nonetheless,
further on, there is an even deeper gloom.
There are no hanged men now:
all of them are on fire.
Could they be made of kerosene inside?
They go on talking,
moving from here to there,
from there to here,
interminably.
Some are sleeping.
Someone is outside.
Somewhere there is sunshine.
Inevitably, the sun exists.
I can no longer leave:
I'll go and sleep.
Inevitably, I'll wake up again.
And so on, and on, and on.
The kerosene burns inexhaustibly.

JORGE VALLS ARANGO, Cuba, 1969
(translated by Emilio E. Labrada and
James E. Maraniss)

The Departed Train

The french horn of the train sighs, weeps a little,
an unattainable myth.
Through the prison bars a match gleam trickles,
the whole world is eclipsed.

The horn takes wing, into the night it sweeps.
To flick through tracks
like notes. Oh how am I to reach
that rainy platform!

Forsaken, sleepless, deserted,
deserted without me –
cloud tatters like letters drift down
to your concrete,

and inscribing the puddles with full stops,
with hooks and tails,
their treble voices ring out after
the departed train.

NATALYA GORBANEVSKAYA, former USSR, 1970
(from *Select Poems*, 1972)

Dawn in the
Great Northern Wilderness

Dawn, and our train will soon arrive.
The deathly silence of prison cars arrests all noise.
All but the fearful, restless clanking of the wheels. . . .
From the windows, glimpsed in the dark night,
black snowflakes flutter over the wilderness.

On the vast plain the white snow
is tramped into a muddy trail,
a long chain of footprints,
still, desolate, cold.

Countless hearts,
prisons for countless wronged souls.
The suffering is great, very great,
but there are no sighs, no groans.

Theirs is the fate
of convicts in a primeval forest.
Axes and saws to cut the year-rings of life.
O, the endless ploughing in the fields!
Ploughshares to crush their shining youth.

Blue light of dawn,
pure, white snow
will bear witness for them:
The suffering was great, very great,
but there were no sighs, no groans.

A long chain
marches into the desolate, deserted snow.

TANG QI, China, 1957
(translated by Geremie Barmé and John Minford)

Transportation

16 August 1969. You, my daughter, are off on your honeymoon in a happy land. And I am off to a happy land somewhere too: I've heard say Buru Island in the Moluccas, an island about the size of Bali. We are supposed to leave tomorrow, if our departure is not postponed for yet another reason. I and eight hundred others will leave on the ship *Adri XV*, a birthday present for the Republic of Indonesia. To board this ship of 300,000 tons dead weight we must first go to Sodong. I'll not close the eyes in my head nor my soul. And the ship will carry me off to the future of my dreams and my beliefs. Buru Island is not the Happy Land, but a way station on the journey: that too requires faith.

The ship's whistle blows and slowly the ship leaves sight of Sodong and Wijayapura. The green of the forests and mountains of Nus Kambangan moves alongside and the white shore gradually disappears from the eye's view. To the south, all that is visible is open sea, the unlimited blue of the Indian Ocean, stretching to the horizon. To the north are the steep and sharply-jagged cliffs of Java's southern coast. Don't listen, shut your ears, to the sound of labored breathing that comes from this rusted, asthmatic ship.

We are sailing just as our precursors did in an age of migration, to discover for ourselves a new land and life. . . . Our ship rocks and shakes. Our cabin is a cell, a forced enclosure, with a huge door of iron bars, locked, as are the doors to the other two cells that are found below deck.

We no longer own our right to look at the sky, or so it seems. We are the coolies. For many of my mates, this journey is their first time at sea, the first time they have ever set foot out of their villages. Most of the men lay sprawled helplessly on mats or on the deck. As the ship enters the open sea, they heave, and then heave some more. One must not stare or laugh at the men whose stomachs are bloated from malnutrition. Many of them have come here directly from prisons where, for a year, their food ration was no more than three shoe-wax tins per day. There's one man who is 160 centimeters but who weighs only twenty-nine kilograms. You have never witnessed the abnormality of a man's bodily movements or that of a man's mental processes whose body weight is less than fifty per cent of what it should be. His huge eyes bulge from their sockets, yet his vision is blurred. His skin is cracked and dry and when he moves, his joints are stiff, like those of the King Kong miniature in the film. As he walks, he looks around, slowly and uncertainly, but he stares blankly and in no certain direction. Even so, as he lies in his own regurgitation, his spirit for life continues to burn.

You have never known real hunger. You are the child of a free people and as a free person you should never have to experience hunger just because of other people's incompetence. But I am the child of a colonized people and if, in my life, I have sustained long periods of bitter hunger, that is not extraordinary.

On this ship, cockroaches patrol, day and night. I sometimes get the shivers and giggle squeamishly when thinking of how those flitting-flying things, those slow-fast moving creatures have successfully gained control over us.

Below deck, ahead of our cell at the very front of the bow is a combination bathroom and latrine. You can't imagine the disgust of the prisoners who must use this place, at least those of us who can still remember the rules of hygiene that were taught us at home and in school. At the entrance to the bathroom-latrine, you immediately slap your hand to your nose and strain not to turn around, for inside the room is a veritable mountain of human faeces. Even without being told to do so, the men in my cell begin to clean that god-awful room. We get out the brooms, barrels for water and then turn the water faucets on. But soon, the pile of faecal matter becomes a muck swamp. The drainage pipes are blocked. Satan himself would have had a hard time finding where the drainage holes were supposed to be. We couldn't believe it. Barrel after barrel of water we poured into that room and still the fetid tidal pool refused to ebb. And as the bow of the ship rose with the waves outside, the liquid excrement of this man-made swamp rolled across the room to lap at and then leap over the low metal divide to flood the cell that had been assigned to us. Ask me, then, if we, the would-be conquerors of this faecal mountain were surprised. Ask me if we were astonished. No! Every place of imprisonment was the same. A hardened mound of shit that started just inside the door and ran all the way to the latrine itself. The only difference is that the floors of the barracks were of earth while the floors of this ship are of rusted steel.

Our ship, with its 300,000 tons of dead weight, continued to wheeze and puff as it made its way forward. We were going fast, about as fast as a leisurely stroll around town on a bicycle. Time and again the ship has stalled, chugged to a stop, to become a bobber on the mid-sea waves. Yes, this is our ship, a ship of the largest archipelago nation in the world!

Supposing that this ship were to sink, we would go down with it, all eight hundred of us, because we are penned up in cells whose doors are all locked from outside. But then, what's wrong with dying? By dying, we would at least be able to give something to the world: a great headline, a sensational story, one that would illustrate the transformation of responsibility into a volley ball. How many creatures, how many types of creatures have been wiped from the face of this earth without eliciting the least bit of fuss?

I can't count the number of times other ships have passed us. From a distance we must be a heart-rending sight, a leper on the course of a bright and healthy life. Every waking moment I am aware of the ship's wheezing and the creaking of its rickety joints. Twice now I've heard the wheezing stop and felt the ship's steel skin shudder as the engine gasped and died.

And yes, there are those who pray. I am sure there are those who pray that a gale-force easterly will sink this ship and that we will die as shark-bait.

Now I, the prisoner of uncertain fate, am surveying this sad world. If you were with me, you too would be amazed by the blueness of the afternoon sky. At night I can see millions of phosphoric dots rising and falling with the waves that strike the ship's keel. This is all I can see from the porthole. No matter where one looks, all that is visible I interpret as signs of death: the sea, the sky, this shit-house ship with its unending creaks and moans, bullets, bayonets, orders, roll calls, rank insignias, hand guns, rifles and camp knives. People say that no matter what you do and no matter where you go, the grave is always your ultimate destination. Whomsoever is born receives at birth a death sentence. Napoleon's journey from Corsica, through the glories of victory on the battlefield, may have given birth to new institutions and codes, but the distance, people say, to Les Invalides, Napoleon's grave, was but a few hundred meters away.

What can I say? Here, in this cage, on this ship, it is difficult indeed not to think about death.

After ten days at sea, the southern coast of Buru Island appeared. Skirting the eastern shore of the island was a unique experience. The island's hills and mountains cluster tightly together, a fierce natural fence that is to be our guard and keeper. Atop the island's baked and cracked soil is a head-dress of elephant grass.

The iron doors are opened. The ship swings round to enter beautiful Kayeli Bay which curves inward towards the coast. The wind blowing from off the shore robs us of our breath and informs us of the island's intense humidity. It carries a warning for us to take especially good care of our lungs and stomachs. There stands Namlea, a natural port on the bay, decorated with small cardboard-like houses. The ship's whistle screams but seeks no quay. The ship is far too large. Two landing craft come out to meet us. A mosque whose minarets stand in stillness and silence peers out from the shore. Namlea looks deserted.

A number of officers emerge from the landing craft and board the ship. A few dozen prisoners, those in the best physical shape, are ordered to disembark first in order to set up a kitchen. Taken away on one of the landing craft, the chosen group of pioneers land on the island. They land at a place bereft of all life, except the squadron of soldiers, who welcome them with rifle butts and fists.

And now you may say to me, Good luck, Papa. For it is your father's turn to leave the ship and board the landing craft, to be taken to this place. A place I have no hesitation in calling Nowhere.

PRAMOEDYA ANANTA TOER, Indonesia, 1969
(from his diary, published in Indonesian in 1995)

Third-class Car 510

Third-class car 510.
The prisoners and guardsmen occupy the first section.
The sergeant hasn't smiled once.
Though the Mausers have been laid on the racks,
     the handcuffs remain locked.
The two sides are in different worlds.

The prisoner Halil opens a book.
He has mastered
     turning the pages
with cuffed hands.
This is his fifth trip
   in thirteen years
      with books and handcuffs.
With lines under his eyes
and white at his temples,
   Halil may look a bit older.
But his books, handcuffs, and heart haven't aged.
And now,
his heart more hopeful than ever,
   Halil sits reading his book
and thinking of his handcuffs:
'Handcuffs, we'll beat your steel into plowshares.'
And he finds this idea so well put
that he's sorry
he doesn't know the art of writing poetry,
measured or otherwise.

The train entered and left the Gebzé station.
It crossed a high iron bridge.
On the right, the earth dropped off sharply
   maybe a hundred,
      maybe a hundred and fifty fathoms,

and there,
   way down
      at the bottom,
the 'Old Fortress' village and castle,
the two horsemen on the long narrow road,
the olive trees, and even the empty sea
looked like toys just out of their boxes
      so small
      and colorful,
so distant
   and deep,
and so quickly left behind
      in the clean spring light.

. . .

The prisoner Halil
closed his book.
He breathed on his glasses to clean them,
   gazed out at the orchards,
      and said:
'I don't know if you're like me,
      Suleiman,
But coming down the Bosporus on the ferry, say,
   making the turn at Kandilli,
   and suddenly seeing Istanbul there,
or one of those sparkling nights
   of Kalamish Bay
      filled with stars and the rustle of water,
or the boundless daylight
   in the fields outside Topkapi
or a woman's sweet face seen on a streetcar,
or even the yellow geranium I grew in a tin can
   in the Sivas prison –
I mean, whenever I meet
   with natural beauty,
I know once again
   human life today
      must be changed . . . '

NAZIM HIKMET, Turkey, 1938–1950
(from *Human Landscapes*, 1982)

Oblivion

At night the moonbeams snap.
The stars are suffocated.
That maligned, unhappy barn owl
screeches out its grief.
The old train on the tracks
hurtles to its destruction
wheezing out its last breath.

And I? I send my thoughts beyond these walls
day in, day out, from dawn to night
(from dawn to night, day in day out)
I dream the endless daydream,
dream the endless journey
through the night, fretting,
champing at the bit:

the one I call for does not come,
the one I wait for never appears
Ah, if I could only stop the
thinking, seeing, hearing, dreaming. . . .

I wouldn't feel a thing.

ZARGANA, Burma, 1988

Dreams in Auschwitz

The light goes out a first time for a few seconds to warn the tailors to put away the precious needle and thread; then the bell sounds in the distance, the night-guard installs himself and all the lights are turned out definitively. There is nothing to do but to undress and go to bed.

I do not know who my neighbor is; I am not even sure that it is always the same person because I have never seen his face except for a few seconds amidst the uproar of the reveille, so that I know his back and his feet much better than his face. He does not work in my Commando and only comes in the bunk at curfew time; he wraps himself in the blanket, pushes me aside with a blow from his bony hips, turns his back on me and at once begins to snore. Back against back, I struggle to regain a reasonable area of the straw mattress: with the base of my back I exercise a progressive pressure against his back; then I turn around and try to push with my knees; I take hold of his ankles and try to place them a little further over so as not to have his feet next to my face. But it is all in vain: he is so much heavier than me and seems turned to stone in his sleep.

So I adapt myself to lie like this, forced into immobility, half-lying on the wooden edge. Nevertheless I am so tired and stunned that I, too, soon fall asleep, and I seem to be sleeping on the tracks of a railroad.

The train is about to arrive: one can hear the engine panting, it is my neighbor. I am not yet so asleep as not to be aware of the double nature of the engine. It is, in fact, the very engine which towed the wagons we had to unload in Buna today. I recognize it by the fact that even now, as when it passed close by us, I feel the heat it radiates from its black side. It is puffing, it is ever nearer, it is on the point of running over me, but instead it never arrives. My sleep is very light, it is a veil, if I want I can tear it. I will do it, I want to tear it, so that I can get off the railway track. Now I have done it and now I am awake: but not really awake, only a little more, one step higher on the ladder between the unconscious and the conscious. I have my eyes closed and I do not want to open them lest my sleep escape me, but I can register noises: I am sure this distant whistle is real, it does not come from an engine in a dream, it can be heard objectively. It is the whistle of the small-gauge track, it comes from the yard where they work at night as well. A long, firm note, then another one a semitone lower, then again the first, but short and cut off. This whistle is an important thing and in some ways essential: we have heard it so often associated with the suffering of the work and the camp that it has become a symbol and immediately evokes its image like certain music or smells.

This is my sister here, with some unidentifiable friend and many other people. They are all listening to me and it is the very story that I am telling: the whistle of three notes, the hard bed, my neighbor whom I would like to move, but whom I am afraid to wake as he is stronger than me. I also speak diffusely of our hunger and of the lice-control, and of the Kapo who hit me on the nose and then sent me to wash myself as I was bleeding. It is an intense pleasure, physical, inexpressible, to be at home, among friendly people and to have so many things to recount: but I cannot help noticing that my listeners do not follow me. In fact, they are completely indifferent: they speak confusedly of other things among themselves, as if I was not there. My sister looks at me, gets up and goes away without a word.

A desolating grief is now born in me, like certain barely remembered pains of one's early infancy. It is pain in its pure state, not tempered by a sense of reality and by the intrusion of extraneous circumstances, a pain like that which makes children cry; and it is better for me to swim once again up to the surface, but this time I deliberately open my eyes to have a guarantee in front of me of being effectively awake.

My dream stands in front of me, still warm, and although awake I am still full of its anguish: and then I remember that it is not a haphazard dream, but that I have dreamed it not once but many times since I arrived here, with hardly any variations of environment or details. I am now quite awake and I remember that I have recounted it to Alberto and that he confided to me, to my amazement, that it is also his dream and the dream of many others, perhaps of everyone. Why does it happen? Why is the pain of every day translated so constantly into our dreams, in the ever-repeated scene of the unlistened-to story?

While I meditate on this, I try to profit from the interval of wakefulness to shake off the painful remnants of the preceding sleep, so as not to compromise the quality of the next dream. I crouch in the dark, I look around and I listen.

One can hear the sleepers breathing and snoring; some groan and speak. Many lick their lips and move their jaws. They are dreaming of eating; this is also a collective dream. It is a pitiless dream which the creator of the Tantalus myth must have known. You not only see the food, you feel it in your hands, distinct and concrete, you are aware of its rich and striking smell; someone in the dream even holds it up to your lips, but every time a different circumstance intervenes to prevent the consummation of the act. Then the dream dissolves and breaks up into its elements, but it re-forms itself immediately after and begins again, similar, yet changed; and this without pause, for all of us, every night and for the whole of our sleep.

So our nights drag on. The dream of Tantalus and the dream of the story are woven into a texture of more indistinct images: the suffering of the day, composed of hunger, blows, cold, exhaustion, fear and promiscuity, turns at night-time into shapeless nightmares of unheard-of violence, which in free life would only occur during a fever. One wakes up at every moment, frozen with terror, shaking in every limb, under the impression of an order shouted out by a voice full of anger in a language not understood. The procession to the bucket and the thud of bare heels on the wooden floor turns into another symbolic procession: it is us again, grey and identical, small as ants, yet so huge as to reach up to the stars, bound one against the other, countless, covering the plain as far as the horizon; sometimes melting into a single substance, a sorrowful turmoil in which we all feel ourselves trapped and suffocated; sometimes marching in a circle, without beginning or end, with a blinding giddiness and a sea of nausea rising from the praecordia to the gullet; until hunger or cold or the fullness of our bladders turns our dreams into their customary forms. We try in vain, when the nightmare itself or the discomforts wake us, to extricate the various elements and drive them back, separately, out of the field of our present attention, so as to defend our sleep from their intrusion: but as soon as we close our eyes, once again we feel our brain start up, beyond our control; it knocks and hums, incapable of rest, it fabricates phantasms and terrible symbols and without rest projects and shapes their images, as a gray fog, onto the screen of our dreams.

For the whole duration of the night, cutting across the alternating sleep, waking and nightmares, the expectancy and terror of the moment of the reveille keeps watch. By means of that mysterious faculty of which many are aware, even without watches we are able to calculate the moment with close accuracy. At the hour of the reveille, which varies from season to season but always falls a fair time before dawn, the camp bell rings for a long time, and the night-guard in every hut goes off duty; he switches on the light, gets up, stretches himself and pronounces the daily condemnation: '*Augstehen*', or more often in Polish '*Wstavac*'.

Very few sleep on till the *Wstavac*: it is a moment of too acute pain for even the deepest sleep not to dissolve as it approaches. The night guard knows it and for this reason does not utter it in a tone of command, but with a quiet and subdued voice of one who knows that the announcement will find all ears waiting, and will be heard and obeyed.

Like a stone the foreign word falls to the bottom of every soul. 'Get up': the illusory barrier of the warm blanket, the thin armor of sleep, the nightly evasion with its very torments drops to pieces around us and we find ourselves mercilessly awake, exposed to insult, atrociously naked and vulnerable. Every day begins like every day, so long as not to allow us reasonably to conceive its end. . . .

I climb down on to the floor and put on my shoes. The sores on my feet reopen at once and a new day begins.

PRIMO LEVI, Nazi-occupied Poland, 1944–1945
(from *If This Is a Man*, 1959)

The Doves

outside doves perch everywhere
it is clear from
their cooings of love and delight
it is clear from
the whirr of their wings
wings which seem to fan me in my prisoner's sleep
it is clear outside
doves perch everywhere

the night is like a day on the other side of the bars
on this side the day is like the night

REZA BARAHENI, Iran, 1973
(from *God's Shadow: Prison Poems*, 1976)

The King of Solitude

Dreams. More strictly, variations on one dream. I would be on the scaffolding of a building in construction, high up. Cold. Mists. The mist barely reveals the outlines of my co-workers on other parts of the building. They are shadowy forms in blurred contours. A relay of hands pass the bricks on to me from the ground. When the last brick is set in place I signal and a new brick flies through the mists, invisible until the last yard or two. But the aim each time is perfect. I catch it with barely a glance, literally by stretching my hand out for the brick to fall into. I place the brick in position, fill the gaps with mortar and slice off the excess. It is hardly work; every movement is leisurely, slowed-down motion, ritualistic. The mists swirl all about us; from time to time a face passes close, balancing on the narrow catwalk, trundling a barrow to another part of the edifice.

It is a long while before I know that everyone else is gone. I did not hear the lunch gong. I could not have suspected it had rung since the bricks continue to drop into my outstretched hands. It is the silence that strikes me first and slowly I realize that work has ceased. The work has proceeded until now in virtual silence but now that silence has grown even deeper. I lean over to ask my own relay if they wish to stop or to continue until that line of the work is completed. Only seven bricks left I say; the figure is always seven. There is no response from them and I notice now that they are also gone. A brick comes flying slowly through the mist though there is no one below. I hold out my hand for it. It slips, I lunge for it and fall over. I am a long time falling in the void.

The little hole in the door is a peep-hole on the living. It sneaks into the yard of Purgatory, the house of lunatics, lifers, violent and violated nerves, cripples, tuberculars, victims of power sadism all safely hidden from questions. The guards thrust their fists through the hole and manipulate the bolt from either side. And I, on my stroll through the yard, casually, oh so casually, steal a quick look at the rare flash of a hand, a face, a gesture in that Purgatory. Alas, too often, all I see is a mere blur of khaki, the square planted rear of the guard on the other side.

Until this morning lying in bed I hear the noise of hammering. All morning the assault of blows is multiplied and magnified by the unique echoing powers of the crypt. (When it thunders my skull *is* the anvil of gods.) I step out to investigate and I find a squad of warders at the gate hacking and sawing and nailing until by noon, the breach is sealed. Only the sky is now open, a sky the size of a napkin trapped by tall spikes and broken bottles, but a sky. Vultures perch on a roof just visible from another yard. And crows. Egrets overfly the crypt and bats swarm at sunset: albino bats, sickly pale, emitting radio pips to prowl the echo chamber. But the world is dead, suddenly. For an eternity after ceasing the hammers sustain their vehemence. Even the sky retracts, dead.

Buried alive? No. Only something men read of.

Days pass, weeks, months. Buoys and landmarks vanish. Slowly, remorselessly, reality dissolves and certitude betrays the mind.

I am alone with sounds. They acquire a fourth dimension in a living crypt, a clarity which, as in the case of thunder, becomes physically unbearable. Pips from the albino bats pock the babble of evensong – Moslem and Christian, pagan and unclassifiable. My crypt they turn into a cauldron, an inverted ball of faiths whose sonorities are gathered, stirred, skimmed, sieved in the warp and weft of sooty mildew on walls, of green velvet fungus woven by the rain's cunning fingers.

Buried alive? I must struggle through the trapdoor of my mind. I must breathe, deeply.

The vulnerable moments are the moments before full awakening, those moments between surfacing to the top layer of awareness and the actuality of climbing ashore. I think of the perilous mornings in terms as this: perhaps too many other consciousnesses hover on a common surface in that hour, too many piles of clothing on the shore and drugged minds drifting in and out without self-markings. If a man in such a state were to pick the wrong clothing, or drift around for ever finding none, all mysteriously vanished. . . .

Each day it takes longer to find my clothes. Odd items stare me in the face, a stained shirt, long underpants, odd sandals. Then I make mistakes and receive odd stares, sometimes a mocking laugh. How long does it last? A flash, as in dreams? Or an eternity? How long has the search taken? How much longer each long day? Whose are the faces dimly recognized? How does a mere metaphor take such real roots? It is not possible to have the same dream dawn after dawn. Perhaps the thought has bred terror and the mind leaps instinctively to the buried fear, timed by approaching wakefulness.

I day-dream back to that lake, returning again and again to my haunted search among alien faces, feet dragging in increasing fear, a fear of error, a fear of waking stranger to myself.

I know the cause. I know the event of some days back whose definition I evade. Plainly it is panic. But the immediate cause? The gate. The nailing in. I diagnose this unprecedented experience: claustrophobia.

Blind, crushing, an overspill of long repressions, a violent uprush of poison fumes in trapped sediments of my insulating capsule . . . suddenly in the dead of night I was forced up from sleep as if my self-capsule had become a mere bubble in the lake of consciousness. The capsule held, refused to burst. I clawed at the smooth surface and begged to let in air. It was a chilly awakening, harmattan night.

The cold intensified the bubble's isolation, panic came in stabs of icy pressure. Why? Why the sudden clogging of my lungs? A wild indiscipline commenced in my pulse, I heard a hammer at my head and my clenched fists became a living thing, a frantic bird pressuring at the closure in the palm. It was pulse, sheer pulse. I felt my heart about to burst, the capsule disintegrate. A herd of stallions thudded at my temples.

May this be borne I asked? My skull is about to burst. The placid lake erupted suddenly and I was lifted clean, plastic cage glass bubble tinsel capsule trapped pinned insect, lifted clean by the eruption and tossed from crest to crest of massive wave ripples. A long arm of the wave caught it in a vicious crook and drew it down again to silt-bed, we slithered from one slimy peak to another. No light, no direction. The lake is an underground cavern, sealed from end to end. There is no handhold within, only a roar in the ears of the vault, a naked earth-core dementia, shrapnels of water making for pulse centres creating disruption.

But you know it for what it is! PANIC! You know it for that alone! IT MAKES NO SENSE!

I heard my own shout and woke. Leapt ashore from the lake surface and made unerringly for my clothes.

But the capsule was sucked in again. And now I had struggled up in bed and sat cross-legged. This is what you want to do I warned: leap up, grab those bars and shake them like a frenzied ape. And scream! For there was this thing, this iron constriction below the heart and breathing had become a torment. And the body was rearing to buck, to leap in flight, smash into the wall and tear it wide open, sweeping down all objects with that inhuman strength which had come upon me. I felt the titanic strength which had come upon me. I felt the titanic strength. It was there! A palpable force. If I let it rule my body even to shifting lightly from that mild restriction of my legs crossed under me, a force was let loose in self-destruction.

WHY? BUT WHY? Are you not master of this environment? Have I not crowned you king of solitude?

Control. Control. Breathe in. Out. Don't let another sound escape you. Hold on to the two parallel bars on the door, your equation marks for those esoteric sciences that keep you busy. Two bars, one equation. Now balance sky to earth, earth to sky. Grip them hard but silently. Touch iron and ram it into your soul. Keep it there.

But when did you arrive at the door?

Earth. Earth. Sit on the floor. Blanket. If only it were not freezing. Pillow then, sit on the pillow to protect your ankles, wrap the blanket around you. Breathe. Itemize all objects beginning with the tooth-brush on the ledge. What is it for? And soap? Count the bars one by one leaving out the equation marks. No, through the nose, breathe only through the nose. All the air you need can come through the nose. Don't pant, you have not been running, hardly room here for that. Don't let the demons in. Now empty your mind. Anchor.

In this cold harmattan night I am covered in pools of sweat. Perhaps after all, it is better to remain in bed, flat. A larger surface is earthed. Arms flat down, heels dug into lumps of kapok, I await the careless moment of this assault, marshalling strength in lucid moments. How describe it? It settles down into a pattern, an acceptable rhythm of ebb and tide, misrule and clarity. A savaging by wolf packs then a brief refuge under an overhang. Fingers on a precipice weakening sickeningly. A long drop in void, a bewildered stillness in the centre of suction. Once I lay flat against a sheer vertical cliff face, held there by nothing but the force which first lifted me onto it. When? I could not tell. A limpet held by the most evenly sinister dis-tribution of force, nothing could prize it loose, there was no gap or the insertion of a wedge of rationality. After each tidewash depth and dimension diminished. Patiently it is washed eroded to a flat sensory plate. Is this my X-ray on the shale?

> Fragments
> We cannot hold, linger
> Parings of intuition
> Footsteps
> Passing and re-passing the door of recognition.

My memory at least proves tenacious. That 'mantra' will serve. Utter words, order moods if thoughts will not hold. Again.

And again. And again. Roll the words in the mouth. Taste wine-grace, pollen flavour, spirit dust. Travel beyond now, let the words prepare their passage, then journey through the passage spreading incense on the way. Dilate the nostrils. Greedily. But greedily! Swallow beyond repletion.

Victory? No, ebb and tide. But one may also be the moon and hold sway over danger, aloft though tossed and ravaged to murky depths. Somehow separate essential self from the twin reflection and make all harrowing phases more sensory sympathy. My shadow is trapped but not my essence. Repeat. My shadow is trapped but not my essence. Now cast a new spell in case of renewed assault:

> Old moons
> Set your crescent eyes
> On bridges of my hands
> Comb out
> Manes of sea-wind on my tide-swept sands.

My liver is mended. I await the vultures for there are no eagles here.

WOLE SOYINKA, Nigeria, 1968
(from *The Man Died*, 1972)

Daybreak

My eyes shut tight, I'm lying sleepless here.
The gong rings loud and long. It's morning now.
I'm lying still, dead still, no thought, no dream,
Just slumbering in shadows, dreary, sad:

shadows of aging parents, dumb with grief,
in a vast night where flicker dots of fire;
the shadows of my life, an empty hush,
deserted, fit for neither tears nor laughs;

the grayish shadows of some wretched loves;
and, tottering to and fro in dark despair,
my own shadow, coughing blood, back-hunched.
I open up my eyes. Stark looms the prison camp.

NGUYEN CHI THIEN, Vietnam, 1969
(from *Flowers from Hell*, 1984)

Letter from a Lunatic Asylum

I am afraid to write to you, my friend Sasha. I fear that you may read my letter as if it's come from a madhouse (as indeed it has, you will shrug). But I have no one else I could write to or of whom I could ask so thoroughly human a favor. You see, I fear even more now that they will use the extra strong drugs on me, turning me into an idiot, who will not even meet his end with a sane mind. So listen to your friend, dear Sasha.

Circumstances force me to write to you in a way I have never written to anyone: this is a letter, not a last will, a necessary explanation not a posthumous postscript – keep that in mind and don't panic.

I am in a very bad way, Sasha. Never have I suffered so much, never has my situation been so hopeless. I have dropped out of society, out of the scope of its laws. I am absolutely without rights, depersonalized, dehumanized. Can you understand? I'm now a 'socially dangerous mental case', as well as being an 'especially dangerous state criminal' and 'especially dangerous recidivist'. There is only one way to escape all these torments, only one way of crawling out of here – that is to betray myself and leave, but no longer as Nizametdin Akhmetov. This route is a barred one, of course, but it means that they will grind Nizametdin Akhmetov down to nothing eventually, on the millstone of 'state security'.

Naturally, I'm not really ill. However, I'm in an institution which has the means of *making* me ill. That is not an exaggeration. Psychiatry has now reached the point physics reached when they split the uranium nucleus. And it is not just one man in a white coat over his military uniform who is against me – behind his back is the entire State. Ah, there's no doubt I'm being ground to pieces! It is horrible, an intolerable alternative torture, this 'treatment'. The 'medicines' they feed and prick me with would be purchased with gusto by Satan in hell. The medieval inquisitors would have given their right arms for them.

Never have I suffered so much.

I am afraid of not bearing up. My will-power is not unlimited. But how could I go on living, despising myself, otherwise?

I know they say I have slandered my country. This is not so, Sasha. I love my homeland, as I love my mother, my house, my people. And if anyone tried to part me from my homeland, to cause strife between us, then let that person be my hangman. . . .

Naturally, I don't have a good relationship with the current regime and ideology. And this leads to the wrong assessments of me. They try to equate my quarrel with the powers that be with a quarrel with my homeland. They are *not* synonymous! One's homeland remains one's homeland regardless of the type of government, monarchy, republic, dictatorship, or democracy; and the real patriot, the genuine citizen, is often persecuted and dishonored . . . I am no nationalist. I am for the genuine and *free* equality of nations and peoples.

If I am in any way guilty before my mother country, then by all means let me be judged by it. But who is my judge now? What kind of great patriotic act is being performed by my being locked away ever since I was 18 and by tormenting me, every hour of the day? It is a pity I will not see the day when my homeland judges me for itself. . . .

The last thing that can happen to a person may well happen to me. In any case, whether I die or am driven mad, it will be the end. The end of a human being. And, if the end is not *humane*, it will still have happened to a human. I want to stress that. For, I would like there to be at least one person who will talk of me, remember me, as a human being.

NIZAMETDIN AKHMETOV, former USSR, 1984
(anonymous translation)

The Burnt out, Disfigured Day

Back beyond the burnt out, disfigured day
I don't remember myself as young.
Unpardoned by yesterday
I look my shadow in the eyes.

I glide beyond the echo of past words
into myself and deeper, as a ghost.
I follow with chill surprise
the shade of dreams I dreamed.

I go to myself as though to a friend,
a dagger behind my back.
And I have no strength, no anger
to come together with my own self.

NIZAMETDIN AKHMETOV, former USSR, 1976
(translated by Richard McKane and Helen Szamuely)

Dream of a Wake

The warders had begun to clink their keys against the bars which separated you, and to knock on the door at the entrance to the visiting room. You had to hurry up and end the visit. You noticed your wife hesitate for a moment. Then her eyes filled with tears and you knew by a slight tremor and pursing of her lips that something was wrong. She turned her head away, unable to stand your questioning look.

'What's the matter?'

'You know, I had something to tell you. I'm sorry I didn't do it sooner.'

'What is it?'

'Your mother is dead.'

'When?'

'The twenty-seventh of July.'

'How did she die?'

'You know she already had high blood pressure. Then she became sort of anorexic. For some weeks she had refused to eat.'

'Why didn't you tell me about it when it happened?'

'Your family begged me not to, to wait until the trial ended.'

'Did you think it would have changed anything in my behavior, had some effect on my morale?'

'No. You know that. But I had promised. Do you forgive me?'

'Yes. Of course.'

The warders brutally pulled the curtain. You had scarcely time to see another tear run down your wife's face. Then nothing. The curtain hid everything. Your eyes were dry.

'Good-bye,' your wife was still saying on the other side of the curtain.

'Good-bye. Don't worry,' you said finally.

You took your basket and went out of the visiting room. In the exercise yard the light was blinding. Your eyes were still dry. There is a feeling of emptiness in your brain and heart, a kind of irritation – as if you had not had and could not have the right kind of reaction. It was true you had learned not to dramatize anything any more. From the beginning of the ordeal you had collected and received so many hard knocks. In its recurrence death no longer had the bitter taste of the destructive unknown. It had become familiar, an ordinary actor in the collective drama.

You returned to your cell with two comrades (at that time you were three to a cell). You took out the food brought by your families. You ate while chatting about the week's events. After drinking tea, each one resumed his place. Each of your comrades got a book out and began to read.

Unlike other occasions, you did not begin a letter to your wife, talking about the visit, so as to prolong the gracefulness of the meeting. You lay down. You unfolded a blanket. You used it to cover your whole body, even your head. Then you opened your eyes in the darkness. You stayed like that for a long time. . . . Quite a bit later – you must certainly have sobbed – you felt a hand being placed on your head. A comrade was calling you. You lifted the blanket.

'What's the matter with you?' he asked. 'Are you ill?'

'Yes. . . No. It's nothing. Some bad news.'

'What is it?'

'My mother is dead.'

At these words, the other left his place and came up to you. He took your hand while the other continued to stroke your head. None of the three of you knew what to say. Silence filled the cell until the moment the warder came round to put out the light. You remained like that in the darkness. Then one of your friends murmured in a quiet warm voice:

'Courage, comrade, courage!'

'Thank you, comrade. I'll be all right.'

Your friends returned to their places. You opened your eyes again in the darkness of the cell which had now become total. Silence reigned, broken from time to time by the noise the rats made scratching the bottom of the bucket which you had filled with water to make it heavy and which you placed over the hole of the W.C. to protect yourselves against these nocturnal pests. The rats knocked against the bucket, got mad, moved it a bit, but could not overturn it. They finally left, hoping to find a way out somewhere else.

You stared into the darkness. You were looking for something. Yes: you were trying to recover the color of your mother's eyes. She had eyes of a particular greenish-blue, more green than blue, like marjoram when it is still fresh.

You can't tell how you fell asleep. A knock-out blow to the head which immediately plunged you into the vortex of a dream.

The scene opens on the small house of 'Ayn al Khayl where you first saw the light of day, where you spent the first days of your childhood. All the neighborhood is gathered to help at a double ceremony. The family is all there. But this is no longer the small clan whose ranks were scattered more than thirty years ago. It's a veritable tribe that parades before you, nephews and nieces, children of cousins, husbands and wives of all that progeniture. Faces you cannot put a name to but who all have what one might call a familiar air.

You are there, in the middle of the crowd, in the splendid clothes of the newly circumcized. You are wearing a green embroidered tarbouch on your head, with a kaftan and babouches of the same color and with the same embroidery. You are enthroned on a chair of painted wood. You pay no attention to the pain which radiates out from your new scar because there's so much going on. In response to the sounds of the *ghaitas* and the wild beatings of the tambours, come the piercing cries of the chorus of wailing women. All around you faces are impassive. They express neither sorrow nor joy. You look in vain for your father in the midst of the crowd. You can't find him.

The wailing women suddenly appear. They come out of your parents' bedroom. But instead of uttering cries, they begin to let out youyous and to recite propitiatory formulas that are only pronounced on happy occasions. They are bearing on their shoulders a mortuary slab on which a corpse is stretched out. They parade around a central courtyard of the house and then put down their burden. Their youyous rise up more beautifully. The *ghaitas* bawl out amid the mad beating of the tambours.

It is your mother stretched out on the slab, rigid, but with a strange beauty. Made up, wearing her bridal dress, she looks as if she has just closed her eyes like any bride during the wedding ceremony. Relatives and neighbors come closer and take out of their pockets banknotes which they wave around ostentatiously before slipping them into the embroidered golden waistband, four fingers wide, around your mother's waist. Each gift provokes more youyous. Finally your father emerges from the crowd.

He is crying. You notice he is the only one who is crying. He goes up to your mother, takes the banknotes and gives them to the woman who appears to be the chief mourner. At the same time the women mourners lift up the slab and go towards the door of the house. Once there, they try unsuccessfully to pass through it but the door is too narrow. They try in every possible way. Nothing works. In a final attempt, they lift the slab up as if it were a wheelbarrow. The body slips and is on the point of tipping out onto the steep road.

You feel your heart beating wildly. You are suffocating. Your body does not obey you any more. It's getting heavier and heavier as if it's being crushed by a gigantic press. You want to cry out and call for help but you can't speak any more. You know that you simply must call out to free yourself from being crushed and to recover the use of your limbs. You struggle with yourself for a long time before you marshal sufficient energy to release your cry. . . .

'Are you all right? Shall I call the warder? Do you want a drink?'

Your comrade goes to the tap in the darkness. You take the water. You drink it and lie down again. . . .

Bit by bit you get your breath back. Your heartbeat recovers its normal rhythm. You lie on your back. You think about your dream. You don't try to decipher it. You look at it as a work of art by the double who lives in your body, ceaselessly weaving the weft of the dark places of your fears and your obsessions. Then a single idea arises from the labyrinth of your terror, a promise. Yes. You promise that the first thing that you will do, if one day you should go free, is to take yourself to the grave of your mother in Fes.

ABDELLATIF LAABI, Morocco, 1972–1980
(from *The Road of Return*, 1982)

Cemetery

The criminal prison autumn
has arrived outside without
our seeing its signs
If we were
in Darakeh now
we could see
the cemetery of yellow leaves
And now that we are not there
we had better put
our heads on the cold tiles of the cell
and sleep until
the sound of shooting startles us
and we rush
to the hole in the cell's iron door
and if the vent is open
watch the silent caravan of the innocent
like Ardaviraf who saw
pre-Islamic hell-dwellers
like Mohammed
who saw post-Islamic hell-dwellers
The identity of the caravan of the innocent
will not be proven in the course of time
Future archaeologists
will remove the firing squad's last bullet
rattling in the empty skull like a peanut
and send it to the laboratory
so that at least
the geological stage of the crime
will be brought to light
And the bald scholars of the future will write
two or three dissertations connecting this peanut
to a dark prehistoric time
which is our present

REZA BARAHENI, Iran, 1973
(from *God's Shadow: Prison Poems*, 1976)

The Executions

Bored as I was, I began, along with a few other inmates, to make worry beads. The dough of the bread was the material we used to form the beads, and we used powdered paint to color them.

At this time, prisoners were being regularly taken for interrogation. They usually wore oversized slippers to these ordeals. The reason for this was that they were regularly whipped on their feet, and in consequence the feet would swell. Had they not taken their oversized slippers, they would have had to walk back to the cell on bare bruised feet.

The daily departure of these prisoners to the prosecutor's office created an incredible atmosphere of terror in the cell. I continued to make worry beads and observe my cellmates. The number of prisoners had drastically increased.

The number of prisoners beaten was also on the rise. I remember well Shahin, a dark-faced girl. She belonged to one of the leftist groups. I asked her to show me her bruises. She laughed and said that because of her dark skin, the bruises could not be seen. I followed each case with avid curiosity. It seemed in some cases that the whole body was one big bruise.

The next night I saw Shahin in the bathroom again. She seemed happy as she chatted to her friend – apparently she had gone to another interrogation, and now felt that the danger had passed. A couple of days later, she seemed rather nervous again: and that night she was summoned once more to the prosecutor's office. The next day, her name appeared on the list of those who had been executed. I had by then become a friend of her friend and I asked her about Shahin. Apparently, Shahin's crime was to have been the driver of a car in the trunk of which a small printing press had been hidden. On the last day of her life, Shahin had told her friend that she thought she was going to be executed. She knew this because the interrogator had fondled her breasts, and that was a sure sign of doom.

The truth is I have never seen a political prisoner who had been sexually abused or molested. There was a rumor that virgins condemned to die were married to the Revolutionary Guards before their execution. According to tradition, if a virgin girl is buried, she will take a man with her. Since no one who was executed ever came back to speak of their experience, I was never able to verify this rumor. Shahin's words are my only proof. I also know of a couple of prisoners who came very close to having sexual relations with their interrogators. In one case the cause was the girl's clever attempt to avoid torture. The second case was a heated love affair between a prisoner and her interrogator.

Toward the end of September, the number of prisoners who could not walk was on the increase. They had been badly whipped on the soles of their feet. After a while a swollen lump, the size of an orange, would appear on the bottom of their feet. One of the biggest problems for these prisoners was walking to the bathroom. Some found a clever solution: they turned a big metal container of cheese into a chamber pot. They installed a thin layer of foam around the rim of the pot; three people would embrace the wounded prisoner and gingerly lower her onto it.

One night, as we all lay in the dark, I decided to go to the bathroom, hoping to avoid the long line in the morning. It was one o'clock in the morning. Prisoners were lined up next to each other on the floor. They were all awake. There was absolute silence in the cell. Something ominous was in the atmosphere. There was no line for the toilet. Instead, a few prisoners stood around and took turns to climb up on the water-heater and look out. When I approached, I saw one of the girls trembling. Although we were not friends, she held my arm and quietly said that the bodies of prisoners were being lined up in the yard. From about eleven o'clock that night, a piercing sound had been heard at more or less regular intervals. One of the prisoners suggested that the authorities were constructing a new visiting center and what we heard was the sound of steel being unloaded. The girl I was with became visibly more shaken when the sound was heard again. I asked *her* about the sound. She said it was machine-gun fire.

By the time that long and bitter night finally passed we had counted more than two hundred and fifty 'coups de grâce'. In the newspapers the next day, I found the names of more than three hundred people who had been executed.

The following day was even more awful for everyone in the block. They took a few prisoners from each block to the office of the prosecutor. There, after summary trials lasting between two and five minutes, the prisoners were divided into two lines. One line was taken to be executed; the other was returned to the cells. The intent was probably to bring terror to everyone. Many of the prisoners who were called to trial that night behaved abnormally for many months afterwards. I saw one of them occasionally fall as she walked, and then get up and continue as though nothing had happened. Another sat the whole night gazing at the toothbrushes, the towels, and the jackets of the executed prisoners. . . .

That same day, they brought Holou to our block. She was a shy girl and stood in a corner motionless. I asked her her name. 'Holou,' she replied. It was a habit of the Mujahadin to give a false name at the time of arrest. In prison, they would call one another by names of flowers, fruits, and animals. The leftists also had the same habit. Holou, Persian for peach, truly resembled her name.

I told Holou that I would like to know her real name. With tears in her eyes, she said she had already died four times. She explained how from the moment of her arrest, up until our conversation, the guards had simulated her execution four times. Twice the Revolutionary Guards had stormed a bus ferrying prisoners, pretending to go on a rampage. On another occasion, they had stood her against a wall, told her she was going to be shot, and then fired blanks at her. I forget the details of the fourth experience. As we talked, it was clear that something *had* truly died in her: she was only fifteen years old and I was filled with silent rage about her torments.

Another of the prisoners, named Golshan, seemed deeply melancholic. I was told that only last week her father, along with other monarchists, had been executed. I tried to help this young girl and soon became friends with her. Before her incarceration, she had performed her prayers religiously, but had quit them upon her arrest. She had been at an engineering college somewhere in England; around Easter time she had returned to Iran to marry her fiancé. Her father was a member of a monarchist group and as bad luck would have it, when Revolutionary Guards raided her father's office to arrest him and other members of the group, she was in the office. As she claimed, and I have no reason to doubt it, her only participation in the group was typing one of their letters. She was arrested along with everybody else. During interrogation she had behaved badly, being utterly intransigent on matters of rather dubious significance. For instance, she had refused to wear a veil or to remove her nail polish from her fingers. The sight of her father's execution changed her radically. I think she tried to compensate for her father's timorous behavior during his trial by her own valor.

While in Evin prison, she had a dream that she related to me. She dreamt that she was engulfed inside an octopus. A big tendril forcefully entered the entrails and plucked someone from inside each organ, placing them in another tendril. Golshan began to scream, 'Take me too! Take me too!' and she ran after the big tendril. The tendril deposited the abducted people on top of a hill and Golshan heard the voice of the Octopus saying, 'I just had this hankering to bring them out here.'

The dream was important. In prison, the killing grounds were called 'hills'. In hindsight, I regret I did not try at the time to analyze her dream for her. I only told her, 'Golshan, be careful.' As was her habit, she took some pills and hid under a blanket. Under the blanket was her only place of solace.

Toward the end of November, overcrowding in the prison reached an explosive point. There were more than three hundred and fifty people crammed in our few cells. Every night, a group of prisoners were forced to stand in a corner, because there was not enough room for everyone to sit down. Summary trials and mass executions had become routine . . . I was tired and disheartened. I felt the weight of all the corpses on my shoulders. In one way, though, I felt happy to be in prison in these treacherous times; I knew that if I were free, and did not take any steps to protest the executions, I would have forever hated myself. But the unfolding catastrophe was much bigger than anything I could do, bigger even than anything a political group could do. In captivity, one is not tormented with these problems, for there is *definitely* nothing one can do. I knew that when the sad history of these days came to be written down, then at least my role would be clear.

Albert Camus, in his interpretation of the Sisyphus myth – the man who had killed his son and was commanded by the gods to spend eternity pushing a rock up a steep hill so that it can roll down again – claims that the man was happy because he need make no choices. Now, in prison, in times of bloody and banal brutality, I too was happy because I need not make any choices. I had not asked to be in this position, but I made no efforts to escape from it, leaving my fate in the hands of the Hezbollah.

SHAHRNUSH PARSIPUR, Iran, 1981
(from an unpublished memoir, translated by Abbas Milani)

141

From the Darkness

From the darkness yonder
Someone is calling me
A pair of glaring eyes lurking in the darkness
The blood-red darkness
Of rusty prison bars.
Silence beckons me
And clogged, halting breath.

On a rainy day of grey lowering clouds
Faltering through the calls
Of pigeons cooing in the eaves
It keeps calling and calling me
A tattered blood-stained shirt
Hanging from the window sill
That red soul which thrashed through endless cellar-nights
the congealed cry of a body racked and torn
Beckoning me
Beckoning me.
The silence yonder is calling me
Calling on my blood
To refuse
To refuse all lies.

From the darkness yonder
On a rainy day of grey lowering clouds
From that darkness of blood-red bodies
A pair of glaring eyes.

KIM CHI HA, South Korea, 1974–1980
(translated by J. de Yepes)

The Suicide

That same evening, after everyone had fallen asleep, I was suddenly woken by a pitiful cry coming from next to me. I sat up quickly and saw the elementary school teacher, hands locked behind his back, bent over the squathole. I realized immediately that this was his second suicide attempt. With his hands fastened behind him, he stood on top of the hole, leapt full-body into the air, and rammed his head onto the cement below, using the weight of his body to smash against the concrete. Everyone was startled awake. Dr Gu went over to lift him up and found blood still flowing from his nose and mouth. On his forehead was an inch-long gash. His pained, blurred eyes were still open, still shining in a face covered with blood. His bloody head rested on Dr Gu's arm and his weak voice was barely audible. 'Don't bother, let me die.' When he finished speaking, more blood came from his mouth. My first thought was that my advice to him to go on living had been futile. Heartless rulers had driven him to death. His last ounce of hope was gone.

Dr Gu's rescue attempt was wasted; the pitiful youth had reached his objective. His beautiful sparkling eyes (I discovered that a dying person's eyes are especially beautiful) closed – very, very slowly.

As before, it was Old Cai who went to the doorway and screamed, 'Guard! There's been an accident!' The guard walked over with sleepy eyes. Hearing that a prisoner had committed suicide, he looked at the door for a while and then, without the least concern, said, 'We'll talk about it at five a.m. Carry the body over here by the door.'

'The dead man still has handcuffs on,' said Old Cai, standing at the door. 'Can't you take them off first?'

With the same indifferent expression, the guard swore, 'You son of a bitch! My orders are that the cell door doesn't open before five a.m. You got that?'

We dragged the corpse to the side of the prison door. His hands were still slightly warm, the glittering KLM electroplated handcuffs cutting into them. He carried with him humiliation, unfulfilled love, the scars of a forced confession, and the censure of his own weakness. ... Perhaps Old Cai was a Christian. He begged the guard to take off the handcuffs, maybe to let the dead man's soul fly up to heaven that much sooner. This unclarified wish was never realized. As far as I'm concerned, once someone is dead, handcuffs won't add to his suffering; his hands may be tightly bound but his soul will not be fettered. The living inhabitants of the cell gathered around the frightening corpse and, sunk in self-pity at our common lot, silently waited for five o'clock. ...

Five o'clock came; the sky was still gray. The guard opened the door and two convict workers came in to haul away the dead man. As they dragged him by the feet like a dead dog, his face turned skyward. The iron door shut and all we heard was the metallic sound of the dead man's handcuffs scraping along the ground. It was a terrible sound, like an iron tool scratching at the pit of my stomach, growing fainter and fainter until it vanished.

WANG RUOWANG, China, c. 1965
(from *The Hunger Trilogy*, 1991)

The Death of Ilhan

Turning to us, the Non-Commissioned Officer said, 'You have even poisoned the minds of ten-year-old kids. The prisons are full of people like you. We get no rest because of you.' As we climbed into the van, they started kicking us and hitting us with their truncheons.

The prison van had two compartments, with a door with a bolt separating them. Four soldiers with truncheons in hand got in and, before the van started, they came to the prisoners' compartment where we were and ordered us to stand up. My brother and I stood at attention and they started to hit our hands with truncheons, two hitting me and the other two my brother. They were lashing out without pity, with all their strength. After a while I started to yell. My brother said nothing. They were kicking, striking and hitting us with truncheons. I saw my brother stumble and fall on the floor. He was having difficulty getting up, but the soldiers went on kicking and beating him. Six years ago my brother had a disc operation.

'His backbone is broken, don't beat him, beat me,' I pleaded.

Nobody listened. Because of the slaps and blows on my face I wasn't able to see my brother properly. It was dark and there were no lights in the van. As we drove off I could see the lights outside through the small barred windows. I again saw my brother being beaten, trying to stand up. I think this beating took half an hour.

The van stopped. They opened the back door and took us out still beating and kicking us. As we were walking towards the prison, we were told to stop. All of them, including the Non-Commissioned Officer, started to beat us again. We were beaten for five more minutes. It was unbearable, and we asked the Non-Commissioned Officer to stop it. He said, 'You should have thought of this before.' Taking his words as encouragement, the soldiers began to beat us more violently. I saw my brother fall again. He couldn't get up. They were on him, kicking, hitting, striking. With difficulty he got up. They told us to stand at attention even though our feet could no longer carry us. Our hands were swollen like logs. We weren't able to keep them at our sides. The Non-Commissioned Officer shouted,

'Keep your hands at your sides, you have only your testicles to worry about.' When the soldiers heard this they started to beat us again. Some time later the Non-Commissioned Officer told the soldiers to stop.

We were taken to the prison gate and went through two barred iron doors. There was a courtyard between this door and the prison ward. As we were walking towards the door of the prison ward, they showed us another door on our right and ordered us to walk that way. When we arrived at the door, they started beating us again. We heard some orders being given. They brought us to the door of the prison ward, still beating and hitting us. My brother fell once more. Then he got up with great difficulty and we stood at attention by the door, two soldiers on each side. Others were yelling from behind, 'Attention, put your hands at your sides.' Three trusties came running, several prisoners took me by the arm, several others my brother. For a moment our eyes met. His face was covered with blood, his eyes were bloodshot.

We looked at each other and said nothing.

My brother took two more steps and said, 'I feel sick, I am going to vomit.' He was about to fall. The prisoners took him by the arm, and laid him down on a bed, taking me inside. They took his shirt off. I saw my brother as they brought him to the bed beside me. There he was, kneeling on one leg, his head lolling, his mouth open.

'Ilhan, Ilhan!' I called. There was no reply.

'Ilhan, Ilhan!' I called again. They told me he would be all right. 'He must have fainted,' I thought. They laid him on the bed just beside me. There was a medical student called 'Doctor' by the other prisoners. He tried artificial respiration.

'My brother is dead,' I moaned.

'No, no, nothing is wrong, his pulse is a little weak, we are trying to help him,' they answered. Fifteen minutes later an officer came and asked for a doctor. After another fifteen minutes, a medical orderly came and asked for an ambulance. They took my brother out on a stretcher. Very tall, he seemed, his mouth open, eyes half-closed. I wanted to kiss him, but the other prisoners didn't let me.

A second later, my brother was gone. He had died right beside me.

There was a cold wind. I was being taken to some other place. I was shivering and about to fall. They wrapped my jacket over my head to stop me from shivering. We walked some 400 meters and came to the officers' casino. The Non-Commissioned Officer who had brought us to the prison was watching television.

'Mr Muzaffer, why didn't you tell us that your brother had a heart problem?'

My brother had no problem with his heart.

Next they took me to a room in section G and put something down on the floor for me. Some prisoners gave me five or six blankets, water and milk. Then the officials came and gave me an injection to put me to sleep.

MUZAFFER ERDOST, Turkey, 1980
(extract from an article in *Index on Censorship*, 1981)

In My Cell

I'm like water
settling down after a shake
letting the foam escape
allowing the sediment to form
filtering out the impurities
on a clear bright morning.

I'm like water
settling down after a shake
look within
at the clarity ringed by mist
the figure appearing in its wholeness
it's no longer just anyone at all

I'm like water
settling down after a shake
the darkness withdraws
the light shines outward:
no longer just for anyone at all

PUTU OKA SUKANTA, Indonesia, 1966–1976
(translated by Keith Foulcher)

Epiphany

It was January, and the frosts which are always linked with the feast of the Epiphany were severe. Tanya, Olya and I decided to observe all the national traditions which accompany this feast. From time immemorial, both in Russia and Ukraine, the custom was to pour water over oneself while standing in the snow, or to dip into a river through a hole cut in the ice. Folk tradition maintains that this will bring good health, and none need fear that it will cause so much as a cold. Our elders, hearing about our scheme, only shook their heads despairingly. Still, they made no serious efforts to dissuade us: if that's what we want, what's the point of arguing? There are times when one moment of pleasure is more beneficial than any medical precautions. Moreover Tatyana Mikhailovna Velikanova, who was old enough to be our mother, always doused herself from the Zone's well on Epiphany, and it did her no harm. We have enough other causes to catch cold: Olya's been in a punishment cell and Tanya and I are in and out of SHIZO all the time.

We were undeterred by the lack of a well in our new Zone. After 'lights out', when all the others had gone to bed, we dragged buckets of water and a tub into the snow outside, and set them down among the drifts. The frost fairly crackled, but the stars were unbelievably bright, and we felt so excited on this special night. We checked the outside temperature with a small thermometer Igor had managed to get smuggled through to me. Not bad. Twenty-five degrees below zero. But our heads are full of intoxicating, youthful daring: nothing can happen to us on a night like this. Our scheme is to strip naked, run through the snow to the buckets and tub, pour a couple of buckets of water over ourselves, then back into the house to dry off and get warm.

Tanya goes first. She runs back, soaking wet and laughing happily. Heavens, even her hair is wet!

I'm next. The snow burns my bare feet, the stars laugh at my protruding ribs, and joy bursts inside me like a small fiery cracker. Here are the buckets. The water feels quite warm. To avoid spilling water on the path (it's my turn to clear it tomorrow) I jump into a snowdrift, and empty the bucket over myself there. After a searing moment, I no longer feel cold. Turning, I run back to the house. Half-way there I am unable to stop myself from waltzing instead of running. Tanya throws a towel over my shoulders. We do not need to look for reasons to laugh this night.

Olya sprints off, and is gone for quite a while. Suddenly, something white and thin raps on the window. It's Olya: she can't find the buckets of water – they had been set out by Tanya and me, and she had run in the wrong direction! Where are they? she asks from outside. Tanya gives her precise instructions, and in a few minutes Olya is back in the house, soaking wet and (we don't believe our eyes) with roses in her cheeks! After drying ourselves, we brew tea. The compassionate duty Cinderella had given us some tea-leaves for the night with the words: 'So that you lunatics can at least get warm when you've finished dousing yourselves!' What we talked and laughed about – I don't remember. Then we recalled that another Epiphany folk custom is fortune-telling: putting mirrors face to face 'to see the future' in them, pouring wax, burning paper and looking at the silhouettes it casts on the wall to see what they resemble.

> Once upon Epiphany eve
> Young girls guessed their futures
> Taking off their little shoes
> Cast them o'er the fence. . . .

We were all staid married women, of course, and instead of 'little shoes' we have only soldiers' tarpaulin boots. Yet I must confess that three such boots were sailing out of the door a minute after we remembered this custom. We know the points of the compass by the sunrises and sunsets. We pull out our old atlas to see where the toes of our 'little shoes' are pointing. Olya's boot points towards Ukraine. Tanya's points to some place east (exile, maybe? Her term expires in the spring) and mine, quite plainly, in the direction of Yavas, where camp Number Two is located with its SHIZO and PKT cells. But this does not diminish our fun. Next, we put two fly-blown mirrors facing each other in a dark room, set out a candle on both sides (all strictly according to the rules!) and peer into the murky corridor of reflected flames:

My destined groom
Come dine with me!

It seemed to me that I saw a movement of something light at the other end. But maybe I was imagining things?

IRINA RATUSHINSKAYA, former USSR, 1982–1986
(from *Grey Is the Colour of Hope*, 1988)

The Spirits of the Book

Superstition is rife in prisons at all times and the magical rituals are handed on by example and experience. . . . Not an hour passed without the presence in our cell of some spirit from beyond. Tired, all our questions exhausted, we pleaded over and over again: Why are we here? Shall we be going home? When will that be?

As I write now, I can smile sceptically, but there, and then, the dark powers of magic made my flesh creep. We used a book to call up spirits of the dead, probably a reminiscence of the missal used in black magic; but for us it did not matter what book it was. It was merely the instrument, but it had to be a fairly light and fairly thin book. You counted the pages and then inserted the handles of two toothbrushes exactly at the middle of the book; the handles had to be flat and straight, and the brush end stuck out at the top and bottom of the spine, bristles upward. They formed the axis from which the book (held shut by a rubber band) hung, and on which it could turn. Two women sat facing each other with the book between them. One was there to address the spirits, the other to help her. Each of them supported one of the brushes on the last joint of her right forefinger. When the spirit had entered the book and began to answer our questions, the book turned smoothly on the taut skin of our fingertips, moving to the right if the answer was YES, to the left for NO. When there was no answer – because the spirit was annoyed by the question or did not know the answer or because the question was not put properly – the book remained motionless.

. . . I can smile at it all now: but inside, I was absorbed by the whole ceremony, and although I was not ready to surrender my disbelief, my scepticism was, to say the least, subdued. I gave myself up to the experience of the moment as wholeheartedly as those who did believe. I trembled all over just as they did; I felt the tension mount as the book turned, manifesting the presence of the spirit; I was moved and spellbound by the ritual. Thinking back to those moments, though, it was perhaps the women themselves who were so moving, rather than the presence of spirits in the cell. Try to imagine them: a cell, grim and gloomy, a comfortless world, indeed a dead world. Homeless souls with the last flicker of hope dying in them. A handful of women, as neat as they can make themselves in their grey rags, sunken eyes with the light extinguished in them, in grey, tired faces. They huddle together in the one corner that is not readily visible from the spyhole. In our atheistic and unspiritual prisons, it is strictly forbidden to have commerce with the spirits. Four, five, six women, six minds each burning not with ten or twelve but a hundred different questions. Raw, aching questions. About lost hopes, broken loves, inaccessible opportunities. About lives that are ruined – as they know too well – and the dead, empty years ahead that are no part of life at all. Is it any wonder that they yearn to find a thread of assurance, of truth, of hope? . . . The living are either inaccessible, or they have already turned their backs. And so these unhappy women call upon the dead.

'Spirit of Vaclav Vojtisek, I call you up from the kingdom of the dead. Come and be here with us.'

There is a moment of tense silence and then the book moves – hesitantly and then decidedly – to the right.

'Spirit of Vaclav Vojtisek, thank you for coming when I called you.'

The book is still, waiting. It is a good thing to be very polite to the spirits, and indeed the ceremonial form of the questions is laid down.

'Spirit of Vaclav Vojtisek, will you answer my questions?'

The book does not move.

'Spirit of Vaclav Vojtisek, I am asking whether you will answer my questions?'

The book moves hesitantly to the right.

'Thank you, spirit of Vaclav Vojtisek. May I put my first question?'

Conversation with a spirit is a ceremonious affair. The book answered again by moving to the right.

We sat in silence, motionless, listening anxiously to the questions. They had to be put clearly; the spirit heard them, and so did we. It was like eavesdropping at the confessional, for each asked about the things that troubled her most deeply. The questions had to be honest and sincerely meant; you can play about with human beings, but not with spirits of the dead. We sat huddled together, living through each other's moment of truth. Strangely enough, none of the secrets revealed in these tremulous moments was ever used as a weapon in quarrels. Even the toughest girls knew that what went on then was sacred, and it was an article of faith that the spirits would take vengeance on anyone who abused the ceremony.

This dark ritual was a plea for mercy, a tempting of fate. . . . One girl, in a daredevil mood, called up the ghost of Adolf Hitler, and then Hitler refused to leave our cell and return to the kingdom of the shades. He resisted all our pleas: Spirit of Adolf Hitler, go back to the world of the dead! The book was unmoved. When that happened, the one who had called up the recalcitrant spirit has to take the book to bed with her and sleep with it. Who can tell what a spirit like that of Adolf Hitler may not do during the night? We were careful not to offend him. In the morning, the girl said she could tell he had gone, because we were all relaxed. The spirits behave in very different ways, some coming readily as soon as they are called, others needing persuasion. But all, without exception, are extremely sensitive to ridicule or offence. If you do not believe in them you had better not call on them.

We huddled together, encouraging each other and prompting the right formulation of the ceremonial questions. . . . Will my trial be soon? In March? In April? Shall I get the hardest sentence? The shortest? Something in between? Shall I be allowed a visit before I'm transferred? Will my husband come to my trial? Will Karel desert me? Will Jan desert me? Will mother look after my little girl? Will they take my apartment away from me? Will they confiscate my savings? Will my husband give evidence against me? Will he divorce me? Will they take the children away from me? Will my children turn against me? Will they stop having anything to do with me? Will the family leave me to my fate? Shall I end up all alone? Will I end up like a stray dog, dead in a ditch somewhere? Shall I get a parcel? Tomorrow? Next week? Shall I get a letter?

Spirit of Vaclav Vojtisek, will there be a general amnesty? Will it be an amnesty for some crimes only? Will it cover what I'm in for? Shall I be in a work camp by then? Shall I still be in jail? Spirit of Vaclav Vojtisek, where shall I be when I'm released?

The spirits were generous. They always said yes to an amnesty.

EVA KANTURKOVA, former Czechoslovakia, 1981
(from *My Companions in the Bleak House*, 1989)

Night

Tall eucalyptus with a broad moon.
A star trembles on the water.
The sky white, silver.
Stones, flayed stones all the way up.
Near the shallow water you could hear
a fish jump twice, three times.
Ecstatic, grand orphanhood – freedom.

YANNIS RITSOS, Greece, 1968
(from *Exile and Return*, 1989)

The Release Order

'We have come to release you.' It is Sunday morning, 29 December, the ninetieth day of my detention. The captain stands in the doorway of my cell, his large bulk blocking out most of the body of a small man in a neat brown suit whom I half see standing behind him. The captain continues:

'Your ninety days are up and you can go now.' I look back at him with suspicion. There is something false in his manner. I say nothing.

The captain moves aside and the short man enters my cell. I recognize him now. He is the colonel, the man in charge of the security forces in Cape Town.

'I am Colonel Macintyre,' he says. I notice that he is holding a piece of paper in his right hand. 'This is for you.' He gives me the paper. His lips mash softly together as he speaks and I observe that his gums are bare. The colonel of the security forces is toothless – no doubt awaiting false teeth.

I take the paper and read it. The words are formal and precise:

. . . is hereby ordered that Albert Louis Sachs who is at present being detained in terms of Section . . . at Caledon Square police station, Cape Town, be released forthwith.

'I think we have met before,' I tell the colonel. 'Weren't you in charge of the police who dispersed the crowd at the "Remember Sharpeville" meeting? In 1961 I think it was.' He had been a captain in the uniformed police then and I remember that he had acted efficiently and with relative absence of provocation to the crowd. I want now to hear the colonel talk a bit more, for from the tone of his voice I should be able to tell whether or not I am really to be released. I do not believe what is written on the piece of paper in my hand.

'That is correct,' the colonel replies. 'You had better pack your things now.' His tone is cool and the words splash quietly from his pouting lips.

'Am I really free?' I ask.

It is the captain who answers. 'Yes, you are really free.'

'You mean I can go home?'

'Yes, you can go home.'

A constable is called to carry my blankets and food. The colonel and the captain push their way out of the cell, which is too small to contain four people, and we all proceed along the passage outside. The steel gate at the end of the passage is unlocked and the procession passes through to the stairs which lead down from the cells to the charge office. I had almost forgotten that my cell was on a level one floor above the ground. When we reach the charge office my belongings are heaped on the counter, and I am asked to sign the receipt for my property.

'Are you going to arrest me again?' I ask as I sign the property receipt.

'You are now completely free,' the captain replies. We all stand quietly, watching each other. The captain looks at my belongings on the counter, smiles warmly at me and says:

'How are you going to get all that stuff home?'

How are you going to get all that stuff home. The sentence echoes through my head and I feel myself tremble. Hope bursts through my defences and swamps over me so that I am overtaken by overwhelming dizziness. Those words can only mean one thing. I am really free.

'You mean I really am free?' The words come faintly from my lips. I feel the pressure of tears on my eyeballs. My hand moves up to my face and my body begins to rock. The captain smiles genially. I want to hug him, and also to kick him.

'I don't know what to say,' I whisper. 'I don't know whether to say thank you or f. . .' I do not finish the sentence. The occasion is too great to be marred with abusive language.

'Can I . . . can I telephone my mother?'

The captain is slightly startled by my request and looks to the colonel. The colonel nods.

'Certainly,' the captain assures me affably. 'The phone is over there. Just wait a minute and we'll get through for you.' I am swooning, I cannot stand. As I seat myself on a bench I notice the colonel walking out towards the street.

I'm free. It's all over.

The colonel returns with Warrant Officer Vlok. The warrant officer walks straight towards me and holds out his hand in greeting.

He is grinning and I see his brown-stained teeth. I stand up shakily and grasp his hand, ready to mumble something about my happiness.

'I am placing you under arrest,' he says.

ALBIE SACHS, South Africa, 1963–1964
(from *The Jail Diary of Albie Sachs*, 1964)

Twenty Years and Forty Days Later

It was about three in the afternoon on 18 June 1984, when we noticed some unusual activity in the officers' headquarters. I was called up. My friends warned me, 'It must be State Security.'

The officer went straight to the point: State Security had come for me and perhaps it had something to do with my freedom. I should take only a towel and a toothbrush – the same baggage they required when you went in for a Treatment. I went back to the cell and told the prisoners within hearing distance what had happened. 'Be careful, it's a Treatment,' one of them warned. Another said, 'And if they really let you go?' I shrugged. I couldn't afford to think about that. My sentence of twenty years had been completed forty days earlier, on 8 May. The next day, 9 May, I had been called to the officer's room. 'You know you have finished your sentence?' he'd said. Sure I knew. 'And you know how things are?' I knew that too. Then we had spoken of different matters.

Today, however, they took me to the director's office. He told me I *was* going to go free. He gave me a pair of trousers, a shirt, and a razor. Something went loose inside me and started to flutter. I cut my face shaving, and got dressed in the new clothes. They took some photos of me, and at sunset, they took me to State Security in Santiago. The officer was trying to be gentle.

'You are free, but tonight you have to stay here with us. If you want, we can take you sightseeing in the city.'

That night, in a State Security vehicle, I was taken out to see Santiago, in polite but rigorous custody. It was near midnight, and I still didn't know what my real situation was. I gazed at Santiago from a hill with several State Security officers. They showed me an amusement park, praising it in their stilted, peculiar style.

'It can handle x number of children per afternoon,' they said. 'It has x number of machines that rotate x number of times per minute.'

The next morning I was taken to Havana by plane. An officer was waiting for us at the airport. We arrived at 'Villa Marista', the State Security headquarters, following a long journey. I was dizzy with a terrible headache and an upset stomach. The officers left me sitting on a bench. Half an hour later, a different official came for me and started treating me as though I were a newly arrested prisoner. They took my clothes away and left me facing the wall. Then they drove me through the building whistling at me like an animal. It was painfully familiar. . . .

They led me to a room where some high-ranking officers were waiting. I entered, angry at the way I had been treated. For several minutes we had a heated conversation. Then we gradually grew calmer – they more than I. They informed me that I was going to be released and would be sent to Caracas on Friday.

Throughout the conversation, I noted that they had accurate information about my family, both inside and outside the country. They said they were interested in taking me to certain places they considered 'achievements of the revolution' before I left the country so I 'wouldn't take away a bad impression of Cuba'. An officer came in to write down my name and personal details for a passport. 'Why do you want to abandon the country?' he asked.

'To breathe,' I answered.

I returned to the first group of officers who asked me if there was anywhere special in the city I would like to visit. I didn't hesitate. 'The University,' I answered. One of the officers smiled. 'I knew it,' he said.

The next day, in civilian clothes, accompanied by two State Security agents, I went to see Lenin Park, Lenin High School, and a model hospital.

We were standing in the park when I saw a little bus painted with black and yellow stripes.

'It's a "zebra",' they explained. 'We're building a zoo where the animals will run free, and people will be able to view them from these buses.'

Then he looked at me and said, 'You know, so they don't live in such inhuman conditions.'

At Lenin High School the principal offered me detailed statistics on how well everything was working. It was a luxurious school with many gardens, museums and playgrounds. I remembered Osvaldo Figueroa's daughter, who was expelled from this same school because her father was a political prisoner who would not accept re-education. I thought of the way it had turned her against her father.

The hospital had such a luxurious lobby that it looked like a first-class Mexican hotel. The three places were indeed attractive samples.

When we got to the University they had the good sense to leave me alone. I walked under the laurels in the plaza and past the columns outside the Rector's Office. I went to the School of Architecture, where I had often gone to see José Antonio Echevarria, a student leader who had been killed in 1957. I wasn't allowed to go in.

I slowly climbed the big stairway and went to the Student Association room. The door was closed. Then I went to the Law School. It was closed too.

'No trespassing,' a voice called from inside. 'Who are you?'

'Don't worry,' I answered. 'I'm just a ghost.'

JORGE VALLS ARANGO, Cuba, 1984
(from *Twenty Years and Forty Days*, 1986)

An Exchange of Prisoners

I didn't even notice how the night had passed. My cellmates were asleep, having covered themselves with their overcoats on top of their blankets. The cell was filled with dense blue smoke – I had been chain-smoking the whole night long. Why was I being such a fool as to worry?

Just think, they'd brought me to Lefortovo and given me a suit. So what? In a while they'd probably start questioning me, and I hadn't slept a wink, like an idiot. Maybe there was still time to get an hour's shut-eye? But as if he'd been listening to my thoughts, the guard opened the food flap: 'Wake up!'

In winter, it's hard to tell the difference between night and morning. It was still dark outside. While we washed and had our breakfast, it began to get a bit lighter.

'Get ready for your exercise!'

They were taking us out rather on the early side, weren't they? It never used to be like that. My cellmates were yawning, they hadn't properly woken up yet. 'You go if you want,' they said. 'We're not going. It's better to go back to sleep.'

I wouldn't have minded half an hour's kip – who knew what was ahead of me? But the door was already open.

'Ready? Come on out!'

'I could do with an overcoat,' I said. 'They've taken my reefer jacket away. I'll freeze outside in just my suit.'

'Right away, right away,' fussed the guard. 'Come with me, we'll find you an overcoat.' He led me through the baths and in the direction of the frisking boxes again. 'Here's an overcoat.'

On a table in one of the boxes lay a brand new overcoat, a hat and something else I couldn't quite make out. The block guard was fussing round me and seemed incredibly nervous, with an unpleasantly unctuous smile on his face. Why was he so obsequious?

I had just put on my overcoat and not yet had time to button it when – click! Mother of God, handcuffs! He had handcuffed my hands behind me, instead of in front. Were they going to beat me, or something? Instinctively I jerked away and jumped back so that he couldn't hit me. That was what the guards always did when they were going to beat you. They would put American handcuffs on you, which tightened automatically at the least movement of the wrists, and then take a running kick at them, so that they tightened up to the limit. It was such agony that you screamed in protest. But a man's absolutely helpless to resist afterwards and you can do what you like with him.

'Easy, easy . . . don't worry, it's nothing, it just has to be done that way.'

An amazingly vile face! But with an ingratiating smile, he stuck a hat and tie on me and buttoned up my overcoat. If it hadn't been for the handcuffs I would never have let him dress me up in this revolting rubbish, which I had never worn in my life.

Yesterday's minibus stood by the porch. Its windows were shuttered. Just off to one side was a police car. The same KGB gents as yesterday got in and surrounded me. We drove for about an hour and a half. Again a police car with a flashing light cleared the way ahead of us. And now I hadn't the least clue where they were taking me, especially when we left the outskirts of Moscow.

'Are the handcuffs hurting you?' asked one of the KGB men from time to time. 'If they tighten up, let us know.'

It is awfully uncomfortable to sit with your arms behind your back.

At last we seemed to have arrived somewhere. We stopped. It was quite light now; it must have been around nine o'clock. The KGB men kept getting out of the car and then coming back in again to warm up. We were waiting for somebody. Cars came and went. I could hear voices and then the roar of engines. An airport?

'Yes. In a minute we're going to put you on a plane. Your mother, sister and nephew will be going with you.'

Strange, this news left me completely unmoved. As if in the depths of my soul I had long since known that this would happen. I had known it and yet kept it from myself – I didn't want to be disappointed. But in actual fact, how else could it all have ended? Wasn't this what they had wanted all the time? The only strange thing was that there were no documents, and they'd said nothing about a decree. I was a prisoner and still had something like six years ahead of me.

It seems odd, after prison, to be able to look to the side. To look over your shoulder and see something new. But you don't remember anything of it, your eyes have got out of the habit. With some difficulty I scrambled up the steps to the plane – it's an extremely awkward thing to do when you've got your arms behind your back. I looked down – cars, a copse, a snow-covered field. An unfamiliar airport, definitely not Sheremetyevo. Later I learned it was an airforce base.

The plane was empty except for me and the KGB men. And again it seemed like a kind of prison, this time with wings.

'Can you take these handcuffs off now?'

'Not yet.'

Their chief officer reminded me of a borzoi dog. The same slightly bulging brown eyes. He was chain-smoking.

'Well, loosen them for a minute, then. I need a cigarette.'

'Give him a cigarette.'

One of the KGB men stuck a cigarette between my teeth and then took it out from time to time to shake off the ash.

'We're just going to take you to the door to show you to your mother and prove that you're already here. Otherwise she refuses to get into the plane.'

Again, I glimpsed the copse, a group of cars, some people, my mother among them. They carried Mishka, my sick nephew, aboard on a stretcher. I hardly recognized him – it was six years since I'd seen him. The lad had grown.

How uncomfortable it is to sit with your arms behind your back. The handcuffs had tightened and were squeezing my wrists. It would be a lot easier if they had handcuffed me at the front. The guard on my right was entertaining me with stories about planes. He told me how many crashes there were a year, and on which airlines. He attentively fastened my safety belt. But I was looking out of the window over the shoulder of another agent, who was as silent as a sphinx. Perhaps I was seeing Russia for the last time in my life? Should I be glad or sorry?

Here in Russia they had done their level best, from my childhood on, to remake me and change me, as if the State had no other care in life. Just think of the prisons and camps they had flung me in, the ways they had found to pillory me! The strange thing was that escaping now from the eternal persecution, I felt neither bitterness nor hatred.

No matter where I went or lived subsequently, my recollections would be unavoidably tied to this land, and such is the nature of memory that it holds no dark, but retains only the bright things. So I ought to be sad, oughtn't I? But no matter how intensely I gazed at the departing, snow-covered earth, I couldn't force myself to be sad.

Of course I would miss my friends who remained behind, and probably the Arbat backstreets and the familiar Russian speech to which my ear was attuned. But I had felt the same about my friends who had already left. And hadn't the dream of my whole life been to visit London? No, none of this was connected for me with the concept of Motherland.

But shouldn't I, then, be experiencing a sense of joy? The joy of victory? No matter which way you looked at it, we had conducted a desperate war against the regime of utter scum. We were a handful of unarmed individuals facing a mighty State in possession of the most monstrous machinery of oppression in the entire world. And we had won. The State had been obliged to retreat. Even in jail we had proved too dangerous for it. Shouldn't I be experiencing the joy of liberation?

I didn't feel joy either, only an incredible fatigue. That's the way it always was with me before a release. I wanted nothing but peace and solitude – and that had been precisely what I never got. And wouldn't be getting now.

My mother kicked up a hell of a fuss with the KGB, demanding to talk with me. Somehow, she had discovered that I was handcuffed. The chief officer with the borzoi eyes appeared and reluctantly permitted a meeting.

Mother was in an absolute rage. 'You are criminals, you are absolute scoundrels!' she cried. 'Even here in the plane you go on tormenting him. As if you haven't tormented him enough all these years!'

The KGB chief frowned in vexation. 'Nina Ivanovna, calm yourself, please.'

All these years my mother had been waging a desperate war against the authorities. She had inundated them with protests, sent open letters to the West, and hadn't given them a moment's respite. Towards the end, in fact, she had been doing everything that I had once done.

Only now, from her, did I learn that I was being exchanged for the Chilean communist Luis Corvalan. What a strange, unprecedented deal! It had happened in the past that two hostile countries had exchanged foreign spies they had caught or prisoners-of-war. But to exchange your own citizens – I had never heard of that before.

Well, what of it? That made two political prisoners less in the world. It was amusing to think that in the eyes of the world the Soviet regime equated with that of Pinochet. This was a symbol of our times.

As for the handcuffs, shouting would never get them off: violence was not the way to obtain freedom. No matter how much you wriggle in handcuffs you only make them tighter. . . .

I stared intently into the canine eyes of the chief officer and he quietly looked away. Dogs and secret policemen can't endure a straight look – I verified that on many occasions. What did he fear most of all in this world? His immediate superior in the service.

'But why, actually, are you keeping me in handcuffs?'

'Well, all right, I'll tell you.' He fidgeted and looked away. 'You're a prisoner.'

'Ah, so that's it! And what will you do when we cross the Soviet frontier? That should happen in about twenty minutes. Over Austria, for instance. Will I still be a prisoner?'

He didn't know what to answer. And the thing that bothered him was not the truth, not international law, but the possibility of a reprimand from his boss. He went into the cockpit to make contact with Moscow, to get instructions.

'Take the handcuffs off him,' he said on his return. And, turning to me: 'Only please, behave yourself properly.'

What was he trying to say? That I shouldn't jump off the plane?

At last I could chafe my wrists and light a cigarette properly. That was better.

'The handcuffs are American, by the way,' said the agent who took them off. He showed me the trademark. As if I didn't know without his help that almost from the very beginning of the regime, the West had been supplying us with handcuffs. . . .

The KGB chief came back again.

'We have crossed the Soviet border and it is my duty to inform you officially that you have been expelled from the territory of the USSR.'

'Do you have some sort of decree or order?'

'No, nothing.'

'And what about my sentence? Has it been quashed?'

'No, it remains in force.'

'So, I'm a sort of prisoner on holiday, on vacation?'

'Sort of.' He grinned crookedly. 'You will receive a Soviet passport, valid for five years. You are not deprived of your citizenship.'

A strange decision that, flying in the face of all Soviet legislation. And they insist that their laws should be taken seriously! They don't even know how to jail or release you properly. A jolly country, never a dull moment!

The plane commenced its final run in to land, and the secret policemen looked down at Switzerland with interest. 'They've got fewer forests than we have.'

'But look how many fields they've got. They're all private here.'

'Everybody here has his own house and his own plot.' It's good, apparently, when there's an 'abroad' in the world, and returning from some service assignment, you can bring the wife some foreign trinkets. Isn't that the highest blessing?

The closer we came to this 'abroad', the more noticeable was the change in the men. That KGB impenetrability and enigmatic reserve melted away. What was left was Soviet Man. There was a certain envy in the looks they gave me – before their very eyes I was turning into a foreigner.

We taxied up to the airport buildings. Suddenly some armoured troop-carriers rolled out onto the runway and soldiers jumped out of them. They cordoned off our plane. 'Huh,' said one of the KGB men sadly. 'That's that. They won't even let us into the airport now.'

Now it was they who were in prison, under armed guard.

An ambulance drove up and took Mishka off to hospital. Then they let mother and me out. We got into a Soviet embassy car. An American car drew up, belonging to Ambassador Davis and we were transferred to it. And that was the entire ceremony of exchange. We never did set eyes on Corvalan, the Chilean communist, or see him get into the Soviet plane.

No search, no checking of documents. A miracle! All my gear, my priceless prison treasures, were lying here too, still in the prison mattress cover, just as I had gathered them up in my cell. Books, notebooks, hidden knives and razor blades, ballpoint pens, refills. Many weeks of life for someone. But none of it had any value any more: in a single instant accustomed values had been turned on their head.

As we drove to the airport terminal, though, I couldn't rid myself of a strange sensation – as if, thanks to a blunder by the KGB, I had carried out something very precious and important, something forbidden, that should never have been let out of the country. Something no search could ever discover.

VLADIMIR BUKOVSKY, former USSR, 1971–1976
(from *To Build a Castle: My Life as a Dissenter*, 1978)

Reveille

In the brutal nights we used to dream
Dense violent dreams,
Dreamed with soul and body:
To return; to eat; to tell the story.
Until the dawn command
Sounded brief, low:
   '*Wstawać*':
And the heart cracked in the breast.

Now we have found our homes again,
Our bellies are full,
We're through telling the story.
It's time. Soon we'll hear again
The strange command:
   '*Wstawać*'.

PRIMO LEVI, Nazi-occupied Poland, 1944–1945
(from *Collected Poems*, 1988, translated by
Ruth Feldman and Brian Swann)

Afterword
Liberated Ruminations

We called our country 'the warm heart of Africa' although we knew that this captured only the tourist truth of the matter. Our country under the President-for-Life was the most autocratic little country ever known. Everything was done for 'security' reasons. We were arrested, charged or not charged, tried or not tried, we were publicly hanged, killed secretly, poisoned or merely *accidentalized*. We were fed to crocodiles. Above all, we were imprisoned: for 'security' reasons. They labelled us 'rebels'. And the only crime we committed to deserve the title was to allegedly break one of the four cornerstones upon which the nation was said by our despot to have been founded: Unity, Loyalty, Discipline, and Obedience.

Technically, we did not need to do anything wrong to be called rebels. Often it was impossible to know when we had crossed the border. The decision was the exclusive privilege of virtually any cockroach who decided to become the interpreter of our President-for-Life. For us to be arrested it only took some character to inform the nebulous authorities that our poem, story, novel or play seemed 'subversive'. It broke the country's law and order, peace and calm, the obvious manifestation of our four cornerstones. And the radio declared that wherever anyone discovered (or invented) rebels, we were to be hunted down like wild beasts and brought to our knees at the nearest police station. There we would be beaten to death or near death. Sometimes we would be disappeared from the face of the earth. Either way, nobody cared. When the authorities sent us to prisons, they professed that everything was for the best. And every prison guard claimed that everything was being done in good faith – for our own security reasons. That was some years ago.

Today, after release and living in exile, the mechanisms for reliving incarceration are virtually non-existent. The pain of our weeping blisters, our flesh glued to the dirty prison clothes; the prison uniform; the humiliating daily searches among our clothes, naked bodies, the cracks of the cell walls, as the guards looked for non-existent pens, pencils, paper, needles and razors; the thankless conferences with inflexible prison officers over prison conditions; our mean efforts to separate fighting inmates, and to hide the quarrels from the guards in order to protect our friends from truncheons, leg-irons and handcuffs: these events and others are reduced to mere disjunctive memories seeking to be effaced.

Having brought into exile a wife and three children, I find the business of survival looms large. We must join the piece work queues like everybody else. Here nobody cares where we have come from or what we have suffered. And why should they? No negative or positive discrimination will be sanctioned. I will probably be the first one to fight it if it is. At any rate, those who have fought for us must catch up on the time they spent doing so. They have done their bit in liberating us. Furthermore, the attempt to assemble those prison silences, the temporal gaps and the blank spaces for the bus, train or market stalls of the world is too elusive. Even imposing on oneself another prison ambience like the 'retreat' as far as that is practicable will not do. The world is too riotous, the milieu too hostile to allow adequate reconstruction of the rarified moments of our detention.

Surviving prison is an art; containing it by artistic reconstruction is probably the engagement of a lifetime; once a prisoner always a prisoner. Once an exile, always an exile.

Let me elaborate. It is difficult now to recapture the many arts of confinement: sitting down because one is denied work; squatting without reading because the only book one is allowed is the Bible (at first only three Bibles for ninety prisoners); sitting without thinking or saying anything to anybody; watching the blank wall expecting to get nothing; counting and recounting the bricks; standing at the door of one's cell after lock-up counting the number of wagtails hanging on one leg, sleeping on the wire mesh which covers the courtyard; fighting over a glimpse of the moon that passes in some direction for only three days in a month; talking to cockroaches; listening to the monotony of the music of mosquitoes or the croaking of frogs outside; speaking to the person in the next cell by tapping the wall; curling up on one's cement floor bed of ragged blankets and reading the smuggled note and newspaper cuttings; watching cobwebs; musing about scorpions as they disappear into crevices; avoiding stinking bat shit that pours like rice from the ceiling into one's mouth; and finally, the art of adopting the prisoner's imposed oral culture and unwillingly rejecting the long established reading culture.

Today, all these arts need special strengths of memory to recapture. To survive imprisonment these negative features of prison existence have to be turned into something positive. To survive life after prison the rule must apply even more viciously. We can afford to stand aside, laugh and perhaps forget temporarily the painful experiences of prison. We can even theorize about them, having been liberated. We can pay homage to the special heroes, like that wonder-warder-courier I am thinking about now.

We should have given him a nobler name. *Noriega*, the nickname the inmates gave him before I arrived, feels too bland to encapsulate the man's daring, his inventiveness, and his abundant selflessness! He was uncharacteristically frail, five foot six, with huge-legged khaki shorts, unevenly starched and creased. He always seemed to shiver in the scorching wind that was trapped in the stinking prison walls. Hanging his head low, he seemed to carry the worn out prison mortarboard uncomfortably. He spelt Fatigue. Now I still see him, his holed boots deliberately squeaking two hundred yards away, to warn us the prison's 'naked-search' is coming.

We would all rush into cell D4 to our heaps of blanket rags and hide whatever proscribed items we had accumulated and which we held dear. Needles, razor blade bits, flattened out toothpaste and dead toothbrushes, crumbs of soap. And especially, newspaper cuttings about foreign campaigns for our release which had penetrated our prison walls mysteriously. Presently, the guards swarmed in, murderous, their truncheons held high. The commander shouted, 'Search! Everybody out! Leave everything inside! Come out naked!' We all trooped out trembling. Naked. We were searched from head to toe, in our hair and under our genitals. They beat our beds, unravelled our blanket rags, trampling them with glee. We stood like helpless chickens in dread.

We sighed with relief when the gang marched out with their red plastic bucket full of whatever contraband materials they could lay their hands on. We ran to put on our prison uniform and remake our beds, cursing at the chaos left behind. Someone swore at the loss of his money, hidden in the hem of his uniform. Another declared his soap gone. As for me, I knew that somewhere among my things

Noriega had hidden a note. We had made a pact that every time I heard his squeaking boots, he was carrying 'explosive material' for me. I found the note, unusually fat: I hid it under my pillow of rags.

At lock-up time, we lined up as they searched us as we entered the cell one by one. Then the commander double-locked the door. After ensuring that the guards were gone, I borrowed the Bible which my friend in the next bed was reading. I lay on my back, knees up, and opened the Book of Amos. Between the leaves, I started the ritual of unfolding Noriega's fat note. I made sure not to rustle the pages. D4 teems with informers.

I found a bulletin of typed world news and two poems by Brecht from David; a note from Pat, with a cheerful summary of the current state of Mercy, my wife, and the children. If I did not come out soon, he said, the German Ambassador had offered to send my son to a private school; John and Veronica were offering to send Lunda, my second daughter, to the secondary school next year. Pat himself was responsible for Judith, my first daughter, who was to start at Our Lady of Wisdom Secondary School. Could my children have grown up in so short a time?

Pat also enclosed two honorary membership cards from International PEN's English and American centres, issued in London and New York respectively. They each bore my name. I had been made a member of PEN. Well, well, well! But I restrained my titillation and avoided too buoyant a mien.

Then there was a note from Landeg in York. He had been travelling giving lectures about me and had even appealed to the headmaster of Eton School in England, supposedly a close friend of our President-for-Life. He talked about my having won the Rotterdam Poetry International Award, received on my behalf by Wole Soyinka. Glory be! Shush!

Then there was a cutting from Britain's *Guardian* newspaper. Lord Almighty! A picture of Ronald Harwood, Harold Pinter, Antonia Fraser, and other members of English PEN reading from my book of poems in protest at the Malawi High Commission in London! It must sure have an effect, I thought. Ten thousand miles away, among the cockroaches of the prison where I lived I felt utterly humbled. Shattered. Such generosity, such warmth I surely did not deserve. All for one slim volume of poems? Why hadn't I written more poems? I was dumbstruck. Despair was vanquished. 'I am belonged,' I heard myself whisper. My friend elbowed me. 'Watch your private bliss! People are watching. And could I have the Bible too, please?' He had been watching me fidgeting blithely. I passed on the Bible at Chapter 1 of the Book of Amos and the lot, just as I would pass on a calabash of frothing beer, while smacking my lips. Soon we were both lost in thought. The commander outside D4 peeped in to ensure everybody was on his bed. He checked the double locks and turned out the light.

That was seven years ago. Now I am struggling with the truncheons of exile. The world outside prison is another dark prison. But I refuse to suckle despair. I have just returned from dropping off my daughters at school. For me to continue to stay here, I have to invent another piece work for next year and get it cleared through the Employment and Immigration departments. The battle for survival continues. For some it never ends.

On one subject I have a clear mind, however: *reconciliation*. The reconciliation with our torturers and with myself now that my country is free. It is a deceptive notion. Some people who are exploiting the new democratic situation think reconciliation means ignoring and forgetting what injuries were inflicted on the psyches of innocent people. I think that someone must reconstruct without fear the stories of thirty years of autocratic rule. I believe firmly that it is the duty of writers to extend the bounds of their imagination in order to reconstruct the moral chaos of the past years. The indignities and humiliation visited on us by that oppressive regime must be reconstructed at all levels, in hopes that future generations do not repeat the destruction of us and our precious resources and energies. Now that tyranny is gone, let aesthetics take over. Let memory artistically repair past injuries. We will not seek to avenge ourselves. Rather we will hope to lay bare the barbarity that human beings are capable of inflicting on others without accountable cause. My aim is to look forward, not back.

It is my fervent hope that such an endeavour will eventually promote that side of humanity which was so magnanimous to me while I lived in prison.

JACK MAPANJE

Biographies

Nizametdin Akhmetov

The Western world first heard of Nizametdin Akhmetov when a desperate letter written by him, and which he hid in a consignment of timber, found its way from his labour camp to what was then West Germany. PEN took up his case as, although arrested at age 18 for his membership in youth movements, he had during his terms of imprisonment become an accomplished poet. In 1983, Akhmetov was moved from the camp to a psychiatric clinic in Alma-Ata. This desperate appeal for help was smuggled out the following year. He was released in 1987 with the advent of *glasnost* and now lives with his wife in the town of Chita to the east of the Urals. The poem 'The Burnt out, Disfigured Day' was translated from Russian by Richard McKane and Helen Szamuely.

Reza Baraheni

Born in Tabriz, Iran, in 1935, Reza Baraheni obtained his doctorate in literature from the University of Istanbul and in 1963 was appointed as Professor of English at Teheran University. He has also taught in universities in the USA and England. He is the author of several novels and short stories and is a celebrated poet. His *God's Shadow: Prison Poems*, (published in English by the Indiana University Press in Bloomington, 1976), are based on a period of 102 days in solitary confinement at the end of 1973, during the time of the Shah. 'The Doves' was originally scratched on the walls of his cell, as he was allowed no paper or pens.

Today, Baraheni lives in Teheran. He is still active in trying to promote democratic liberties in his country and was a signatory to a 1994 open letter to the government of Iran calling for artistic freedom and an end to censorship.

Czeslaw Bielecki

Born in 1948, Czeslaw Bielecki is a Polish architect and writer. He was an active member of political opposition groups from 1970 onward and the founder of an underground publishing house called CDN ('To Be Continued'). He was first arrested while still a student in 1968. Imprisoned briefly in 1983, he was re-arrested in 1985 and charged with attempting 'to abolish the communist order by force'. He was released in a general amnesty in 1986, after eleven months of detention. He now lives in Warsaw.

Breyten Breytenbach

Born in 1939 to a poor Afrikaans background, Breyten Breytenbach established himself as one of the leading poets of the avant-garde 'Sestigers' group. He left South Africa in 1959 and spent much of the next decade in Paris writing and painting. In exile he became increasingly political in his outlook, and he entered South Africa clandestinely in 1975. He was arrested under the Anti-Terrorism Act and sentenced to nine years in prison. He was released in 1982 and returned to Paris, where he still lives. The extract printed here is from his memoir, *A Memory of Sky*.

Joseph Brodsky

Born in 1940 in what was then known as Leningrad, Joseph Brodsky began to become known for his poems as early as 1958, when Anna Akhmatova, the doyenne of Russian poets, declared him to have exceptional promise. He was not a member of the officially controlled Soviet Writers' Union and therefore found it virtually impossible to have any of his poems published officially. During his time in the USSR, he was sent twice to psychiatric institutions for examinations and, in 1963, he was arrested, charged with 'social parasitism' and sent to a remote camp to undergo five years' hard labour. After serving eighteen months, however, he was allowed to return to Leningrad. He was forced into exile in 1972 and subsequently lived in the USA. In 1987 he won the Nobel Prize for Literature. In 1991 and 1992 he served as Poet Laureate of the United States. His collections of poetry and essays include *A Part of Speech*, *To Urania* and *Less Than One*.

Joseph Brodsky died on 28 January 1996, a few weeks after writing the foreword to this book.

Dennis Brutus

Born in 1924, Dennis Brutus is a pre-eminent poet who has campaigned against racism throughout his career. He was born in what was then Rhodesia (now Zimbabwe) but went to live and work in South Africa, where he taught in high schools for fourteen years. His successful campaigning to exclude South Africa and Rhodesia from the Olympic Games led to his being banned from all political activity and, in 1963, he was arrested. He escaped while on bail, but was arrested again, shot while making a further escape attempt and sentenced to eighteen months of hard labour. Brutus now lives and works in the USA.

The two poems printed here are from *A Simple Lust*, published by Heinemann in 1973.

Vladimir Bukovsky

Born in 1943, Bukovsky was first arrested while still a student at Moscow University for participation in student demonstrations. He was expelled from the university in 1961 for organizing a poetry reading in Mayakovsky Square. In 1963 he was sent to jail for his *samizdat* writing and at one point confined in an insane asylum. He was one of the first to smuggle documents to the West regarding psychiatry abuses in the USSR. In and out of detention repeatedly through the 1960s and 1970s, he was finally expelled in 1976. Bukovsky now lives in England. The extracts printed here are from his memoir, *To Build a Castle: My Life as a Dissenter* (André Deutsch, 1978), translated from the Russian by Michael Scammell.

Angel Cuadra

Angel Cuadra Landrove, a poet, was born in Havana in 1931. He served as the legal representative of the Cuban Writers' Union and was also a member of the Society for Culture and Literature in Matanzas. His first collection of poems was published both in Cuba and abroad. An associate of Fidel Castro against Batista, Cuadra later adopted a more critical stance towards Castro. In 1967 he was arrested and accused of having worked against the security of the State. He was released in 1982 after serving a fifteen-year sentence in full. Three years later he emigrated to the USA. A substantial selection of his poetry and essays (*The Poet in Socialist Cuba*) was published in English translation in 1994. The poems printed here were written in prison and translated by Donald Walsh.

Milovan Djilas

Milovan Djilas spent a total of twelve years in prison, in the royal jails of pre-war Yugoslavia in the 1930s, and under the communist regime of Tito. He served as a vice-president of the former Yugoslavia, but fell from grace in 1954 because of his uncompromising defence of democratic freedoms. He was expelled from the Communist Party in 1954 and arrested in 1956. He authored four volumes of personal memoirs, short stories and novels. The two extracts printed here are from *Of Prisons and Ideas*, published in the USA by Harcourt Brace Jovanovich in 1986. The translator is Michael Petrovich. Milovan Djilas died in April 1995.

Muzaffer Erdost

Muzaffer Erdost, a poet, essayist and publisher from Turkey, was detained along with his younger brother Ilhan (also a publisher), in

Ankara in November 1980. The two were accused of possession of left-ist books by such writers as Engels and Lenin. On 7 November, the two brothers were brutally beaten up by their military escort and Muzaffer saw his younger brother die as a result of the blows to his head. Five soldiers were later charged with the murder. Today Erdost lives in Ankara.

Ruth First
Ruth First was born in Johannesburg in 1925. During the 1940s, she was one of the few whites who supported the black cause. She edited several radical newspapers, exposing the miserable labour conditions of black workers on farms and down the mines. She was a close associate of Nelson Mandela and Walter Sisulu. A member of the African National Congress and of the South African Communist Party, she was arrested and detained in 1963 under the ninety-day law, which allowed the police to hold anyone under suspicion for ninety days without charge or trial. She was released only after 117 days, much of which was spent in solitary confinement. Her book about the experience, *117 Days*, from which this extract is taken, was published by Penguin in 1965.

On her release, First left South Africa. She wrote *Barrel of a Gun*, about African *coups*, and *The Elusive Revolution*, about Libya. She lectured in sociology at Durham University, England, and then moved to Mozambique, where she was a director of research at the Centre for African Studies. She was murdered by a letter-bomb in Maputo in 1982.

Izzat Ghazzawi
Izzat Ghazzawi, a Palestinian, was born to a refugee family on the West Bank in 1951 and started writing while still a student at the University of Jordan. He also studied at the University of South Dakota, USA. He was imprisoned by the Israeli administration from 1989 to 1991 for membership of a then illegal organization. The extract printed here is from *Point of Departure: Letters from Prison*, the English publication of his Arabic *Letters Yet to Be Delivered*, and was translated by Khalil Touma and Lesley Abu Khater.

Natalya Gorbanevskaya
Natalya Gorbanevskaya was born in 1936 and educated at Leningrad University. Throughout the 1960s, her poetry was published in *samizdat* journals. In 1968 she signed a series of prominent letters in defence of intellectual dissidents who had been arrested; in August of that year she participated in a peaceful demonstration in Red Square against the Soviet invasion of Czechoslovakia where she was arrested but quickly released, as she had a child of three months with her. In 1969 she was a

founding member of the action group for the Defence of Civil Rights. She was arrested later that year and sent to Butyrka prison. In April 1970 she was diagnosed as a schizophrenia sufferer. She was held in various hospitals of confinement for the next three years, although her friends and colleagues were convinced that the diagnosis was false. She became known in the West when Possev-Verlag, a Frankfurt publishing house, published a collection of her verse in Russian. The poem printed here was taken from a collection edited and introduced by Daniel Weissbort (*Select Poems by Natalya Gorbanevskaya*, Carcanet Press, 1972). In 1975 she emigrated and has since lived in Paris. In 1990 her poems began to be published in Russia.

Dashiell Hammett
A popular writer of mystery fiction, including *The Maltese Falcon*, Hammett was born in 1894 and grew up in Philadelphia and Baltimore. He left school at age 14 and eventually found work as a detective for Pinkerton's Agency. He began writing after the First World War and by the 1920s was the undisputed master of mystery writing in the USA. He married the playwright Lillian Hellman. During the McCarthy era, many intellectuals were accused of 'un-American activities', or communist sympathies. Many were blacklisted and some were imprisoned. Hammett was imprisoned for a few weeks during 1951. The two letters printed here to his daughter Josephine were sent from his prison cell. Hammett died in 1961.

Vaclav Havel
Vaclav Havel was born in 1936. He is President of the Czech Republic and an internationally acclaimed playwright. He was sentenced to four and a half years' imprisonment in 1979 for his work with Charter 77, a human rights group advocating democratic change. In January 1983 he was released for health reasons. While imprisoned he wrote letters to his wife, Olga, once a week, which were collected and published in English in 1987 in a translation by Paul Wilson.

Nazim Hikmet
Nazim Hikmet, a Turkish poet, was born in 1902. He was in and out of prison several times from adulthood on, but his longest stretch in prison started in 1938 when he was charged with inciting the army to revolt and convicted on the sole evidence that military cadets were reading his poems. He was sentenced to twenty-eight years in prison, but released after twelve years in 1950. These years in prison affected his poetry radically, and formed the base for his novel in verse, *Human Landscapes*, which

appeared in English in 1982. *Human Landscapes* was begun in 1941, when Hikmet wrote from prison, 'I am writing 50 lines a day.' Halal, the political prisoner, scholar and poet featured in the extracts printed here, is going blind. He is usually assumed to be one of Hikmet's many fictional *alter egos*. The translators are Randy Blasing and Mutlu Konuk.

In 1950, Hikmet went into exile, were he spent the last few years of his life living in Sofia, Warsaw and Moscow. He died in 1963.

Eva Kanturkova

A prominent Czech author, Eva Kanturkova spent most of the year 1981 in prison for her alleged activities 'against the interests of the Republic'. She was a signatory and supporter of Charter 77, a human rights declaration and group of the same name, which advocated democratic freedom for former Czechoslovakia. Her novels were banned until the overthrow of communism in 1989. She lives in Prague.

The extract printed here comes from *My Companions in the Bleak House*, a memoir about her imprisonment published by Quartet Books (London) in 1989 and translated by a friend of the author who preferred to remain anonymous.

Kim Chi Ha

'I'm not a Solzhenitsyn, you know. I'm Kim Chi Ha. Not a tragic figure. A comic figure, with these bad teeth of mine. I feel happy in most situations. But the chance to write freely, that's what I hope most for now. The chance to write freely.'

Kim Chi Ha, one of South Korea's pre-eminent poets, was born in 1941. He was arrested in 1964 while still a student, and again in 1970 after publication of his poem 'Five Bandits'. A third arrest occurred in 1972, and in 1974 he was arrested a fourth time, accused of supporting the Federation of Democratic Youth and Students, which allegedly organized demonstrations against the regime, and sentenced to death. The sentence was commuted to life imprisonment in the face of an international outcry, and he was released in 1980.

He is author of the anthologies *Yellow Earth* and *Cry of the People*. The first piece printed here, an extract from a poem called 'Groundless Rumors', is from the latter collection, which was first published in English in 1974. The translators wished to remain anonymous. The second poem, 'From the Darkness', was translated by J. de Yepes and appeared in English in the magazine *Index on Censorship* in 1975.

Today Kim Chi Ha lives and writes in Seoul.

Kim Dae-jung

A South Korean writer and politician, Kim Dae-jung spent several periods in prison or under house arrest. In 1980, he was imprisoned and sentenced to death; the letter printed here was written while he was still expecting to be executed. An intensive international campaign on his behalf led to his sentence being remitted and to his eventual release. On several occasions he has sought political office and ran in the presidential elections of both 1971 and 1987. His letters from prison have been published in Japan, Korea and the USA. The letter printed here was translated by Choi Sung-il and David R. McCann.

Arthur Koestler

Arthur Koestler was born in Budapest, Hungary, in 1905, educated in Vienna and imprisoned in Spain in 1938, where he was condemned to death. International protests on his behalf, including those by PEN, secured his release. He was also imprisoned in France in 1940, and on escaping to England he joined the British army. His novel *Darkness at Noon* (1941) won him international fame. The extract printed here is from *Dialogue with Death*, a play based on his experience of facing what seemed like certain execution.

Arthur Koestler committed suicide in 1983.

Abdellatif Laabi

Abdellatif Laabi, a poet, spent eight and a half years in a Moroccan prison for 'conspiracy against the state'. He was born in Fes in 1942 and published his first novel, *L'Oeil et la nuit* (*The Eye and the Night*), in 1969. He was arrested at his home in Rabat in 1972, tried in August the following year, and sentenced to ten years in prison. He was held until 1980. After his release, he wrote *Rue du retour* (*The Road of Return*), a memoir about both his time behind bars and his return to his family on his release. It is written entirely in the unusual form of the second person. The English translation, from which the extract printed here is taken, is by Jacqueline Kaye. Today, Laabi lives in France.

Primo Levi

Italo Calvino hailed Primo Levi as 'one of the most important and gifted writers of our time'. Born in Turin in 1919, he was both a chemist and a writer. He joined an anti-Nazi group in northern Italy and, in 1944, was arrested and transported to Auschwitz. He was sent to work in the laboratories, which was probably why he survived. He continued to work as a chemist until his retirement. He was author of, among other titles, *The Periodic Table*, *The Drowned and the Saved*, and *If Not Now, When?* He was also a celebrated poet. *If This Is a Man*, his extraordinary account of his time in Auschwitz from which the prose extract printed here is taken, was first published in Italy in 1958. The translation into English is by Stuart Woolf. His poem 'Reveille' was written in 1946 and translated into English by Ruth Feldman and Brian Swann.

Primo Levi died in 1987. He is believed to have committed suicide by jumping down a stairwell in his home.

Osip Mandelstam

Born in 1891, Osip Mandelstam is one of Russia's greatest poets. Like Pasternak and Akhmatova, his life and work testified to the exigencies of living under Stalin's regime. The poem featured here was written while Mandelstam was serving a spell of internal exile. He had been arrested in 1934 for having written a poem which ridiculed Stalin's taste for torture and execution; someone informed on him. Perhaps as the result of the intervention of his literary friends, he escaped execution and was sent first to the Urals and then to Voronezh, where his wife was permitted to join him. The prison experience marked him so profoundly that while in the Urals he attempted suicide. For the rest of his life he lived constantly on the edge of nervous and physical collapse. The couple returned to Moscow in 1937. Mandelstam had two heart attacks, but his ill-health did not prevent his re-arrest in 1938. He was sentenced to five years' hard labour for 'counter-revolutionary activities'. It is reported that he went insane in captivity. He died in 1938, *en route* to a Siberian labour camp.

George Mangakis

George Mangakis, born in 1923, worked as a law professor at Athens University. He was dismissed from his job by the military regime in 1969 and a few months later was imprisoned and tortured. He received an eighteen-year sentence. He was sent into exile in 1973. This extract is from his *Letter to the Europeans*, written from his prison cell. Today he lives in Athens.

Jack Mapanje

Jack Mapanje, one of Africa's most distinguished modern poets, was formerly head of the English Department at the University of Malawi. His collection, *Of Chameleons and Gods*, was published by Heinemann in 1982. A second collection was in the offing when he was arrested in September 1987 and held without charge or trial for over three and a half years. He was released in May 1991 and now lives in York, England.

Mapanje once told a PEN officer that he had found himself unable to write in prison. However, in exile, he has started writing again. The poem featured here was first published in 1992. His collection, *The Chattering Wagtails of Mikuyu Prison*, was published in 1993 by Heinemann's African Writers Series. He is currently working on a memoir.

Anatoly Marchenko

Anatoly Marchenko was born in 1938 in western Siberia, the son of illiterate railway workers. He was first arrested in 1960, escaped, and was re-arrested while trying to slip across the border into Iran. He was sentenced to six years in the camps. On his release he wrote *My Testimony*, from which the extract that appears here was taken. After the KGB learned of his writing activities, he was hounded and spent much of his remaining life in the gulag, where he died in 1986 age 48. *My Testimony* was published in the West by Pall Mall Press, London, in 1969. It was translated by Michael Scammell.

Ngugi wa Thiong'o

Ngugi wa Thiong'o is arguably Kenya's best-known writer. He writes in both English and his native Gikuyu. The author of the novels *Weep Not, Child*, *The River Between*, *A Grain of Wheat* and *Petals of Blood*, he was arrested in 1977 and detained without charge or trial. It is thought that his detention sprang from a recent staging of a play in Gikuyu he co-wrote called *I Will Marry When I Want*, which is thought to have been frowned upon by the Kenyan government. He was released after a year, but found himself under constant scrutiny by the authorities. He emigrated and now lives in the United Kingdom.

Ngugi's prison notes were published in 1981 under the title *Detained*. The book referred to in the extract, which was confiscated and then returned to him, was eventually published in English under the title *Devil on the Cross*.

Nguyen Chi Thien

Nguyen Chi Thien, a poet from Vietnam's north, has spent most of his adult life in re-education camps. He was born in Hanoi in 1933 and by the time he reached his twenties was actively contributing to independent journals. His individualistic ways and outspoken opposition to communism caused him to be imprisoned from 1958 to 1960, from 1962 to 1964 and from 1965 to 1978. In 1979, Nguyen managed to gain entry into the British Embassy and deposited there a manuscript of poems entitled *Flowers from Hell*. The poems had been composed in his head in detention and written down on his release. For this action, he was again arrested and released only in 1991. The two poems printed here were translated by Huynh Sanh Thong. Nguyen Chi Thien left Vietnam in 1995 and now lives in the USA.

Nien Cheng

Educated in London, and the widow of an official of the Chiang Kai-shek regime that was overthrown by the communists in 1949, Nien Cheng was targeted as 'a corrupt element' during the Cultural Revolution in China, which began in 1966. That year her home was ransacked, and she was arrested the following year. She was held for more than six years. During this time she was held in solitary confinement and handcuffed as a punishment for refusing to 'confess' to her faults. When she was released she discovered that her only daughter had met her death at the hands of the Red Guards not long after her arrest.

Nien Cheng's gripping account of the Cultural Revolution and of the years she spent in prison was published first in the UK in 1986 by Grafton Books under the title *Life and Death in Shanghai*. Today, Nien Cheng lives in the USA.

Shahrnush Parsipur

Shahrnush Parsipur was born in 1946. Her first novel, *The Dog and the Long Winter*, was published in Iran in 1974. After the 1979 Iranian revolution, reprints of it were forbidden. Another of her novels *Tuba and the Meaning of Night*, has sold over 50,000 copies in Iran. She is also a prolific short story writer. She was arrested in 1981 and held until 1986. In 1990, following publication of a book of short stories entitled *Women without Men*, she was re-detained for sixteen weeks. Another brief arrest occurred in 1991. Most of her works are banned. Today, Shahrnush Parsipur lives in the USA. The translator of her unpublished memoir about her time in prison, from which an extract appears here, is Abbas Milani.

Alicia Partnoy

Alicia Partnoy, born in 1955, was among 30,000 Argentinians who disappeared after the military *coup* in 1976. At the time of her arrest in 1977 she was a student of literature, clandestinely collecting and disseminating information about the repression. She was also married with a one-year-old child. While in prison for nearly three years she smuggled out stories and poems, which were published anonymously. On her release, she was reunited with her husband and child and now lives in the USA. Her book about her experiences as a blindfolded 'disappeared' person, *The Little School*, from which these extracts come, was published by Virago Press in 1988. Partnoy varies her tales between first and third person and sometimes assumes the persona of other detainees.

Molefe Pheto

Molefe Pheto was active in Soweto's Black Arts community. A founder member of MDALI (Music, Drama, Arts, Literature Institute) and its first chairman and spokesman, he was opposed to apartheid in the arts. His first novel, inspired by the shooting of a civilian by the police, was confiscated before it could be published. Pheto was arrested for being an alleged communist in 1975. He spent a total of 282 days in jail, all but ten of them in solitary confinement. He was then tried, found 'not guilty' and released.

His book about his detention, *And Night Fell*, from which the extract printed here is taken, was published by Heinemann's African Writers Series in 1983.

Pramoedya Ananta Toer

Pramoedya Ananta Toer was born in Central Java in 1925. He was imprisoned in a Dutch colonial jail from 1947 to 1949, during which time he composed some of his major early works, including the novel *The Fugitive*. In 1965, the army began a violent campaign against all those suspected of having communist sympathies. Hundreds of thousands were killed, and many others were sent to prisons and camps. Pramoedya was also arrested, and was held between 1965 and 1979. Most of this time was spent on the notorious Buru Island, a detention centre where many met their deaths. Pramoedya composed a quartet of novels while detained there, all of which have been translated into English.

The extract printed here is from Pramoedya's diary entry for the year 1969, when he was transported by boat to Buru. It was published in Indonesia in 1995 under the title *The Silence of the Mute*, but was quickly banned. The diary is due to be published in the USA by William Morrow & Co. The translator prefers to remain anonymous.

Putu Oka Sukanta

A poet and short story writer originally from Bali, Putu Oka Sukanta was arrested in 1966 along with many of Indonesia's left-leaning intellectuals. He served ten years in appalling conditions in Jakarta's Salemba Prison and Penjara Tangerang in West Java. The poem printed here is from his collection *Tembang Jalak Bali (Song of the Starling)* and was translated by Keith Foulcher. Today, Putu works as an acupuncturist, a skill he learned in prison, and is still unable to publish his works freely in Indonesia.

Irina Ratushinskaya

Born in Odessa in 1954, Irina Ratushinskaya was arrested in 1982 for 'anti-Soviet agitation and propaganda' on account of her writings in *samizdat* magazines. The following year she was sentenced to seven years' hard labour and five years' internal exile. She was sent to a camp in Barashevo, Mordavia, and held with other women prisoners of conscience in a part of the camp known as 'the small zone'. While imprisoned she secretly wrote several poems, some on bars of soap with burnt matchsticks. These were smuggled out to the West. PEN was the first to publish a collection of her work abroad, in a trilingual edition (Russian, French and English). The translators of the poem which appears here are Richard McKane with Helen Szamuely (published in *Pencil Letter*, Bloodaxe Books, 1988).

Ratushinskaya was released in October 1986, on the eve of the Reykjavik summit meeting between Mikhail Gorbachev and Ronald Reagan. Her memoir of her imprisonment, *Grey Is the Colour of Hope*, was published in a translation by Alyona Kojevnikov and the extract entitled 'Epiphany' is taken from this work. She now lives in England with her husband and twin children.

Yannis Ritsos

Born in 1919, Yannis Ritsos was one of Greece's most prolific poets. From 1934 on, he published about a hundred books of poetry, translations, essays and dramatic works. Ritsos, a communist, was jailed for four years in the late 1940s and was arrested again after the 1967 *coup* which brought the military to power. He was detained in camps on Yiaros and Leros, and then sent into exile on Samos, where he lived under house arrest until freed in 1970. Ritsos died in Athens in November 1990.

The poems he wrote during the military dictatorship were rarely political in content. The two printed here, however, are among the few which refer to his imprisonment. They were translated by Edmund Keeley and are part of a collection of his poems entitled *Exile and Return*.

Albie Sachs

Albie Sachs, born in 1935, was a young barrister working in Cape Town, South Africa, when he was arrested on 1 October 1963 and held without charge or trial in solitary confinement for 168 days because of his anti-apartheid activities. On his release, he wrote an account of his detention, *The Jail Diary of Albie Sachs*, which established his reputation as a writer and was adapted into an extremely successful play by the playwright David Edgar. He also wrote *The Soft Vengeance of a Freedom Fighter*. After emigrating from South Africa, he became a professor of law in Mozambique and while there was, like Ruth First (see above entry), a victim of a letter-bomb. Unlike her he survived, although he lost an arm as a result. In a 1990 Preface to a new edition of his jail diary he writes, 'The freedom struggle needs intimacy and softness as much as it requires firmness. . . . This was my little contribution towards recording what it was like in those days of suffering and hope.'

Ken Saro-Wiwa
Ken Saro-Wiwa was executed by hanging in Nigeria on 10 November 1995. He was arrested the previous year and charged with incitement to murder. The underlying reason for his arrest and conviction was his outspoken opposition to Nigeria's successive military governments and his defence of the Ogoni tribe, of which he was a member. The Ogonis live in Nigeria's south, on land that has been environmentally degraded by intensive oil extraction by multinational companies.

Ken Saro-Wiwa was one of Nigeria's most beloved writers. Poet, novelist and screenplay writer, his work won both critical and popular acclaim. His novel *Sozaboy* was hailed by British writer William Boyd as one of the 'finest achievements of African literature'.

Varlam Shalamov
Born in 1907, Shalamov was a prose writer and poet who was sent to Kolyma in north-eastern Siberia for seventeen years, ten of them merely for declaring the Nobel Prize laureate Ivan Bunin, who was out of favour, a 'classic author' of Russian literature. On his release, Shalamov wrote *Kolyma Tales*, based on short episodes of prison life. His work has often been compared to Chekhov. Solzhenitsyn asked him to co-author *The Gulag Archipelago*, but Shalamov refused, pleading ill-health and old age. He died in 1982. The translator of *Kolyma Tales*, from which the extract printed here is taken, is John Glad. (The book is available as a Penguin Twentieth-century Classic.)

Ahmad Shamloo
Born in about 1928, Ahmad Shamloo is one of Iran's most respected poets. Among his poems are 'The Game Is Over', published shortly before the fall of the Shah, and his collections include *A Poem, That Is Life*. He has been in trouble both before and after the 1979 revolution that brought the Ayatollah Khomeini to power; he has been arrested, forced into hiding or into exile on more than one occasion throughout his career. Today he lives in Teheran and, like Reza Baraheni above, has signed a declaration calling for an end to censorship. The poem 'Punishment' was first published in Farsi in 1959, in a volume entitled

The Garden of Mirrors. The translators are Ahmad Ebrahimi and Karina Zabihi.

Alexander Solzhenitsyn

Born in 1918, Alexander Solzhenitsyn is author of many novels and the immense memoir *The Gulag Archipelago*, from which the extract 'First Cell, First Love' is taken. *One Day in the Life of Ivan Denisovich*, from which the extract 'Breakfast in the Gulag' is taken, is a fictionalized account of life in a Siberian labour camp. Solzhenitsyn spent many years in such camps. He was first arrested in 1945 and charged with making slighting remarks about Stalin. Released on Stalin's death in 1953, he taught in a secondary school and began his writing career. He fell out of favour in the late 1960s and was expelled from the Soviet Writers' Union in 1970, the same year that he won the Nobel Prize for Literature. After many years in exile in Vermont, USA, Solzhenitsyn returned to Russia in 1994.

Wole Soyinka

Wole Soyinka, novelist, poet and playwright, was born in 1934. He was arrested in 1967 and held until 1969 because of his outspoken opposition to the Biafran war and his criticism of the military government. In prison, he jotted down notes between the lines of books which his friends smuggled in to him. On his release, he wrote up the notes and the resulting book was first published in London in 1972 by R. Collings under the title *The Man Died*. In 1986, Wole Soyinka won the Nobel Prize for Literature. Today, he lives in exile and gives lectures all over the world. He is extremely active in promoting the cause of democracy in today's Nigeria, which is still ruled by the military, and was a champion of the executed Nigerian writer Ken Saro-Wiwa (see entry).

Tang Qi

Born in 1920, Tang Qi was one of the most promising of modernist Chinese poets in the 1940s. He wrote very little between 1949 and 1980. The poem chosen here, 'Dawn in the Great Northern Wilderness', was written between 1957 and 1958 during the Cultural Revolution and is based on the transportation of trainloads of political undesirables into the bleak, undeveloped areas of north-east China. The poem was translated by Geremie Barmé and John Minford, the editors of *Seeds of Fire: Chinese Voices of Conscience*, the book from which it is taken.

Jacobo Timerman

Jacobo Timerman was born in Ukraine, but moved to Argentina at the age of five. He worked as a journalist, founding two weekly news magazines, and in 1971 became editor and publisher of the influential daily *La Opinion*. In 1977, during the so-called 'dirty war', when thousands of Argentinians were abducted, and often killed, by the army, Timerman was arrested. He was held without charge or trial and tortured, and was released after thirty months (four months of which were spent in various prisons, twenty-six under house arrest). Timerman then emigrated to Israel and now lives in Tel Aviv. His account of his detention, *Prisoner without a Name, Cell without a Number*, from which the extracts here are taken, was translated from the Spanish by Toby Talbot.

Judith Todd

Judith Todd was a prominent critic of the Ian Smith regime which ruled what was then Rhodesia (now Zimbabwe). She wrote articles and gave speeches, both at home and abroad. In 1971, she returned to Rhodesia after five years spent living abroad. Her request for a British passport (which would have afforded her protection) was turned down. She was arrested on 18 January 1972 along with her father, a former prime minister of the country, and detained without charge or trial for five weeks. She was then released but kept under house arrest. While in detention she went on a hunger strike in protest at being held for no crime other than that of expressing her views.

Her book, *The Right to Say No*, which she wrote while under house arrest, was published by Sidgwick & Jackson, London, in 1972.

Cesar Vallejo

Born in Peru in 1892, Cesar Vallejo graduated in literature and was one of the most illustrious poets of the twentieth century. In November 1920, he was arrested and wrongly accused of planning a riot. He was jailed until March 1921, during which time he continued to work on a major poem. As well as revising old poems, he composed new ones – one of which is featured here – about the prison experience. Two years after his release he left Peru for Europe. He died in Paris in 1937.

Jorge Valls Arango

Jorge Valls Arango was born in 1933 near Havana. When Batista carried out his *coup* in 1952, Valls became involved as a student in the struggle against his dictatorship. Persecuted and imprisoned, he went into exile but after his return – and with Castro now in power – he was re-arrested. In 1964 he was sentenced to twenty years in prison for his admitted opposition to Castro's regime. Refusing to accept political 're-education' in return for better treatment, he served out his sentence in full, plus forty extra days. On his release, Valls was forced to leave Cuba immediately. He emigrated to the USA where he now lives.

His book *Twenty Years and Forty Days*, a prose account of his prison ordeal, was translated by the author with Anne Nelson. The poem, 'Where I Am There Is No Light', was translated by Emilio E. Labrada and James E. Maraniss.

Wang Ruowang

Wang Ruowang, born in about 1917, is a satirical essayist who has had three spells in prison throughout a long career of dissent. The extract about a hunger strike, 'Peanuts and Sesame Cakes', is based on a period of imprisonment between 1934 and 1937, when Wang, aged seventeen, was arrested by the Guomindang for his membership of the Chinese Communist Party. Wang was subsequently re-arrested in the 1960s during the Cultural Revolution, and the extract about the suicide is based on this period of detention. He was also detained in 1989 for his support of the Tiananmen Square Democracy Movement. Wang now resides in New York City.

Both extracts are taken from *The Hunger Trilogy*, which was published in China in 1980. The book was translated by Kyna Rubin with Ira Kasoff and published in the USA by M. E. Sharpe, Inc. in 1991.

Zargana

Zargana, which means 'tweezers', is the pen-name of Maung Thura. Born in 1962, Zargana is a poet, humorist, actor and dental school graduate. He was arrested in 1990 after reportedly impersonating one of Burma's military leaders before an audience of thousands in a stadium in Yankin and sentenced to five years. He was sent to Rangoon's Insein jail, a prison notorious for its poor conditions. He was freed in March 1994 and continues to live in Burma. The translator of Zargana's poem 'Oblivion' has asked to remain anonymous.

Zhang Xianliang

Born in 1936, Zhang Xianliang is considered to be one of China's greatest living writers. He is author of the novels *Getting Used to Dying* and *Half of Man Is Woman*. Zhang has spent a total of twenty-two years in Chinese prisons and labour camps. Whenever possible he kept a diary, which was terse and cryptic so as to protect him in case of its discovery. His memoir *Grass Soup*, from which the extracts printed here are taken, was based on some of these diary entries, but was written ten years after his release. It was published in the USA in 1994 in a translation by Martha Avery.

Permissions

Grateful acknowledgement is made to the following authors, publishers, translators, heirs and agents for their permission to reprint poems or extracts in *This Prison Where I Live*.

Every effort has been made to trace the copyright holders of each extract included in this anthology. Any omission is unintentional, and the publisher would be glad, if notified, to make due acknowledgement in any future edition.

Czeslaw Bielecki Extract from *Letter to the Boys – 1985 to 1986*. Reprinted by permission of the author.

Breyten Breytenbach 'Seasons and Storms', from *A Memory of Sky*. Reprinted by permission of the author.

Dennis Brutus 'Colesberg: En Route to Robben Island' and 'On the Island', from *A Simple Lust*, published by Heinemann Educational Books Limited, London, 1973. Reprinted by permission of the author.

Vladimir Bukovsky From *To Build a Castle: My Life as a Dissenter*, translated from the Russian by Michael Scammell and published by André Deutsch, London, 1978. UK and Commonwealth (excluding Canada) rights granted by André Deutsch, London. All other world rights granted by permission of the author.

Milovan Djilas Extracts from *Of Prisons and Ideas*, copyright © 1984 by Milovan Djilas. English translation copyright © 1986 by Harcourt Brace and Company, reprinted by permission of the publisher. Translated by Michael Petrovich.

Muzaffer Erdost Extract from 'The Death of Ilhan', published in *Index on Censorship*, London, 1981. Reprinted by permission of Sol ve Onur Yayinlari, Ilhanilhan Kitabevi.

Ruth First Extract from *117 Days*, first published by Penguin Books, 1965 (reprinted 1982). Reprinted by permission of Jonathan Clowse Ltd, on behalf of the estate of Ruth First.

Izzat Ghazzawi 'Marwa, My Daughter', from *Point of Departure: Letters from Prison*, published by the Arab Center for Contemporary Studies, Jerusalem, 1993. Reprinted by permission of the author.

Dashiel Hammett Personal letters held by University of Texas, Austin. Reprinted by permission of the Literary Trustees and the Harry Ransom Humanities Research Center, the University of Texas, Austin.

Vaclav Havel 'Halfway Mark', from *Letters to Olga*. English translation by Paul Wilson. First published in English in the USA as *Letters to Olga: June 1979 to September 1982* by Alfred A. Knopf Inc., New York. First published in the UK by Faber and Faber Ltd in 1988. Reprinted by permission of the author.